Web Research in Academic Libraries

CLIP Note #41

Complied by
Rebecca Sullivan
Assistant Professor, Academic Technology Librarian
Preus Library
Luther College
Decorah, IA

College Library Information Packet Committee
College Libraries Section
Association of College and Research Libraries
A Division of the American Library Association
Chicago 2010

The paper used in this publication meets the minimum requirements of the American National Standard for Information Sciences-Permanence of Paper for Printed Library Materials, ANSI Z39.48-1992.

Library of Congress Cataloging-in-Publication Data

Web research in academic libraries / compiled by Rebecca Sullivan.
    p. cm. -- (CLIP note ; #41)
  Includes bibliographical references and index.
  ISBN 978-0-8389-9926-4 (pbk. : alk. paper) 1. Electronic information resource literacy--Study and teaching (Higher)--United States. 2. Internet literacy--Study and teaching (Higher)--United States. 3. Internet searching--Study and teaching (Higher)--United States. 4. Library orientation for college students--United States. 5. Library surveys--United States. I. Sullivan, Rebecca. II. Association of College and Research Libraries. College Library Information Packet Committee.
  ZA4065.W43 2010
  025.04071'173—dc22
                        2010031944

Printed in the United States of America.

14 13 12 11 10   5 4 3 2 1

Cover design by Jim Lange Design

TABLE OF CONTENTS

       Lynchburg College
       Knight-Capron Library
       Lynchburg, VA

       St. Catherine University
       St. Catherine University Libraries
       Minneapolis/St. Paul, MN

Fairfield University
DiMenna-Nyselius Library
Fairfield, CT

Elon University
Carol Grotnes Belk Library
Elon, NC

University of St. Thomas
O'Shaughnessy-Frey Library
St. Paul, MN

York College of Pennsylvania
Schmidt Library
York, PA

Northern Kentucky University
W. Frank Steely Library
Highland Heights, KY

Tarleton State University
Tarleton State University Libraries
Stephenville, TX

College of Mount St. Joseph
Archbishop Alter Library
Cincinnati, OH

Louisiana State University at Alexandria
James C. Bolton Library
Alexandria, LA

Search Engines and Directories 55

Winthrop University
Dacus Library
Rock Hill, SC

Southern Oregon University
Lenn and Dixie Hannon Library
Ashland, OR

Tarleton State University
University Libraries
Stephenville, TX

Dakota State University
Karl E. Mundt Library and Learning Commons
Madison, SD

Tufts University
Tisch Library
Medford/Somerville, MA

University of Colorado at Colorado Springs
Kraemer Family Library
Colorado Springs, CO

SUNY College at Oneonta
James M. Milne Library
Oneonta, NY

Northwestern College
Ramaker Library
Orange City, IA

Search Strategies   81

Grinnell College
Burling Library
Grinnell, IA

Gustavus Adolphus College
Folke Bernadotte Memorial Library
St. Peter, MN

Southern Oregon University
Lenn and Dixie Hannon Library
Ashland, OR

Springfield College
Babson Library
Springfield, MA

Tufts University
Tisch Library
Medford/Somerville, MA

Neumann University
Neumann University Library
Ashton, PA

Missouri Western State University
Missouri Western Library
St. Joseph, MO

Assumption College
Emmanuel d'Alzon Library
Worcester, MA

SUNY Plattsburgh
Feinberg Library
Plattsburgh, NY

Randolph-Macon College
McGraw-Page Library
Ashland, VA

Tufts University
Tisch Library
Medford/Somerville, MA

Widener University
Wolfgram Memorial Library
Chester, PA

University of St. Thomas
O'Shaughnessy-Frey Library
St. Paul, MN

Tarleton State University
University Libraries
Stephenville, TX

Elon University
Carol Grotnes Belk Library
Elon, NC

St. Catherine University
St. Catherine University Libraries
Minneapolis/St. Paul, MN

Eckerd College
Peter H. Armacost Library
St. Petersburg, FL

Widener University
Wolfgram Memorial Library
Chester, PA

Western New England College
D'Amour Library
Springfield, MA

Springfield College
Babson Library
Springfield, MA

Dakota State University
Karl E. Mundt Library and Learning Commons
Madison, SD

Bucknell University
Bertrand Library
Lewisburg, PA

Bowdoin College
Bowdoin Library
Brunswick, ME

Springfield College
Babson Library
Springfield, MA

St. Catherine University
St. Catherine University Library
Minneapolis/St. Paul, MN

CLIP Notes Committee members

Erin T. Smith, Lead Editor
McGill Library
Westminster College
New Wilmington, Pennsylvania

Gillian S. Gremmels, Chair
EH Little Library
Davidson College
Davidson, North Carolina

Sharon M. Britton
Library
Bowling Green State University - Firelands College
Huron, Ohio

Jennie E. Callas
McGraw-Page Library
Randolph-Macon College
Ashland, Virginia

Rachel C. Crowley
Logan Library
Rose-Hulman Institute of Technology
Terre Haute, Indiana

Lynda Duke
Ames Library
Illinois Wesleyan University
Bloomington, Illinois

Janet S. Fore
Cushwa-Leighton Library
Saint Mary's College
Notre Dame, Indiana

Lawrie H. Merz
Murray Library
Messiah College
Grantham, Pennsylvania

Christopher Millson-Martula
Knight-Capron Library
Lynchburg College
Lynchburg, Virginia

Debra Cox Rollins
James C. Bolton Library
Louisiana State University at Alexandria
Alexandria, Louisiana

Kathryn K. Silberger
James A. Cannavino Library
Marist College
Poughkeepsie, New York

Doris Ann Sweet
Emmanuel d'Alzon Library
Assumption College
Worcester, Massachusetts

Nancy J. Weiner
David and Lorraine Cheng Library
William Paterson University
Wayne, New Jersey

With gratitude to Craig and Pram.

INTRODUCTION

Objective

The College Library Information Packet (CLIP) Notes publishing program, under the auspices of the College Libraries Section of the Association of College and Research Libraries, provides college and small university libraries with reviews and documentation of current practice and policy. This *CLIP Note* provides information on teaching Web search strategies in information literacy instruction.

Academic use of the Web is a comparatively recent concept. Professional journals in the 1990s commonly published articles about introducing the Internet and teaching first-time users how to navigate a Web browser, and there was an early emphasis on partnering with faculty to encourage the use of Web sites in the curriculum. Now, in a more complex electronic environment, undergraduates gravitate to the Web for their information needs. To what extent and in what ways have academic libraries incorporated Web search strategies into their information literacy instruction?

Literature Review

In 2002, The Pew Internet Project and an OCLC White Paper demonstrated that most college students use the Web, and particularly search engines, as a primary resource for their research (Jones and Madden 2002, OCLC 2002). In fact, Pamela Martin argued that Google has had a formative effect on the way students search, influencing them to skim, prefer keyword queries, and expect a simple process (2006). Although undergraduates have confidence in their ability to navigate the Web, Deborah Grimes and Carl Boening revealed that a gap exists between faculty expectations and the quality of resources students use (2001). Susan Davis Herring found that, as a result, faculty tend to limit use of the Web for assignments (2001). Nicholas Tomaiuolo showed that the majority of faculty prefer that students use subscription databases, but that open Web use prevails (2005). Likewise, the Project Information Literacy Report "How College Students Seek Information in the Digital Age" reported that nearly all students turn to Google for their research needs, second only to course readings. The report concluded that students are driven to the Internet "by familiarity and habit," despite frustration with "finding relevant resources, sorting through too many results from online searches, and evaluating the credibility" of information (Eisenberg and Head 2009, 32).

Following one of the many citation studies that demonstrate student use of the Web, Philip Davis suggested that librarians can influence student scholarship by encouraging faculty to set clear Internet guidelines as a means to ensure that students practice evaluating online sources (2003). A study by Carol Wright found that libraries are increasingly directing students to Web resources with links to search engines, annotated subject guides, and evaluative criteria on their library Web sites (2004). Although an OCLC White Paper recommended that libraries point to quality Web resources to help students discern which sites are suitable for academic research, Caroline Cason and Anna van Scoyoc cautioned that if Web resources are consistently displayed on course sites, students may not learn search or evaluation strategies for themselves (2006).

In addition to highlighting the importance of teaching students critical thinking skills to evaluate Web information, the literature places a priority on teaching Internet search strategies. In 2003, Susan Colaric led an empirical study of three instructional methods for teaching users how to search the Web, concluding that effective instructional design on Web searching may increase relevant results and decrease user frustration. Christen Thompson recommended that lessons on the use of Boolean operators and advanced search features be integrated into library instruction on the Web (2003). Tony Fonseca and Monica King demonstrated the value of showing students the results of different permutations of Web searches: promoting "basic skills such as narrowing or expanding a search; adding, eliminating or combining terms; and varying the search vocabulary and spelling" (2000). However, in 2008 Konstantina Martzoukou argued that it may be more productive for librarians to focus on motivational aspects and student attitudes toward the effectiveness of structured searches (2008).

More recently, some colleges have accepted Google Scholar as a useful resource on the open Web. In 2005, Maurice York discussed how, after some deliberation, libraries are integrating Google Scholar into their sites as a discovery tool (2005). Karen Hartman and Laura Bowering Mullen documented the implications of putting Google Scholar on the library Web site (2006), while David Ettinger argued that librarians must come to terms with Google Scholar as they endeavor to teach students its pros and cons (2007).

Along with clarifying the features of search engines, librarians can introduce students to directories and the invisible Web. Francine Egger-Sider and Jane Devine advocated guiding students to the diverse tools that access the invisible Web to locate information that lies beyond search engines (2005). In "Using the Invisible Web to Teach Information Literacy," Mary Hricko reported on using the invisible Web to help students develop information literacy competencies as defined by ACRL standards (2002).

In terms of structuring instruction, Laura Cohen maintained that search instruction should derive from a user's information need and should emphasize concepts rather than specific search tools (2007). Judith Arnold and Elaine Anderson Jayne compiled recommendations to "use active learning techniques, such as hands-on practice, team teaching, and the use of student-centered classrooms in which instructors serve as coaches or facilitators" (1998). Bradley Tolppanen emphasized that search techniques cannot be taught all at once, but should be staged based on students' development and proficiency (1999). Finally, Shinichi Monoi, Nancy O'Hanlon, and Karen Diaz measured how mastery experiences have an impact on students' self-efficacy which, in turn, becomes an indicator of student performance and success (2005).

Survey Procedure
The author used the standard procedure for *CLIP Note* surveys. After the initial proposal and draft of the survey were submitted to the ACRL College Libraries Section's *CLIP Notes* Committee for approval, electronic surveys were sent to participants in October 2009. A reminder was sent in December 2009 and responses were accepted until January 2010.

ANALYSIS OF SURVEY RESULTS

Surveys were sent to 215 college and university libraries. A total of 118 libraries responded to the survey, representing a response rate of 55%. Slightly more than half of the respondents shared documents, teaching materials, and Web sites related to library instruction on searching the Web.

While 25% of the respondents were public institutions, 75% were private. Enrollments were grouped as follows:

Fewer than 2000 students – 38%
2000 to 3999 students – 30%
4000 to 5999 students – 21%
More than 6000 students – 12%

The majority of these libraries still operate as independent units (58%), although 30% are part of a larger entity and 10% are merged with information technology. The number of librarians at these institutions ranged from 2 to 29 (FTE), teaching from 589 to 15,000 students.

Frequency and Format (Questions 8-9)
Respondents' most common response (45%) to the frequency of their instruction or assistance on searching the open Web was one or more times daily. At institutions with FTEs over 6,000 students, an even higher percentage, 69%, teach Web searching on a daily basis. Twenty-two percent of all institutions reported that librarians teach or assist students concerning Web searching several times a week, while 20% teach these skills every week or two. Only 6 respondents reported that they provide Web instruction or assistance rarely or not at all. There is a pattern in this data: the percentage of libraries dwindles as the responses indicate less frequency in teaching Web searching.

Ninety percent of respondents pointed to one-on-one assistance as the most common format for teaching about the Web, often at the reference desk or in individual research appointments (fig. 1). Along with the traditional settings for one-on-one instruction, some libraries indicated that they also offer individual assistance via instant messaging and e-mail. Other libraries reported roving the library labs as the impetus for one-on-one research assistance.

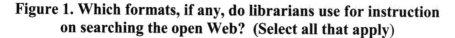
Figure 1. Which formats, if any, do librarians use for instruction on searching the open Web? (Select all that apply)

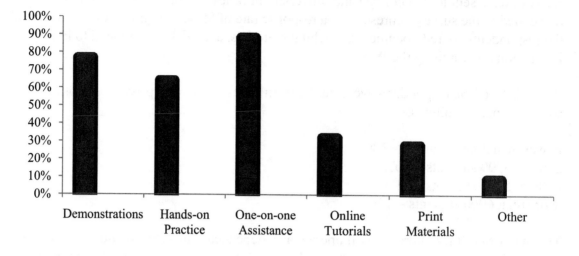

Demonstrations	Hands-on Practice
One-on-one Assistance	Online Tutorials
Print Materials	Other

Seventy-nine percent of respondents offer demonstrations and lectures, some incorporating PowerPoint or student presentations. Sixty-six percent include hands-on practice in their lessons. Nearly all (98%) of respondents have a facility to offer hands-on instruction in the library building. Sixty-four percent also have suitable space in another campus building, and 41% offer hands-on sessions using laptops in a wireless environment. Only two libraries reported that they do not have access to a computer facility for hands-on instruction; just one said that librarians do not choose to use a hands-on format.

Roughly a third of responding librarians, mostly from larger institutions, rely on online tutorials—designed locally or linked to other sources—for instruction on the open Web. About the same number distribute print materials, such as course-specific research guides.

Context (Question 10)
The greatest number of librarians, 83%, have taught sessions on the Web in the context of specific courses, sometimes at the request of an instructor. More specifically, 52% have taught the Web in first-year programs and 40% in instruction for senior projects/theses. A lesser but still significant percentage, 27%, have introduced Web concepts in library orientation sessions. An additional 18% have discussed the Web in credit-bearing library courses.

Three respondents pointed to faculty development workshops and "faculty library sessions" as contexts for discussion about how to do research on the Web. Some respondents commented that practices among librarians at the same institution vary because they don't share a set curriculum for the instructional program. Although only formal instructional contexts were included in the question, seven respondents still identified the reference desk as a common setting for Web instruction.

Formulating Searches (Questions 11-14)

Reflecting the prevalence of one-on-one instruction in the area of Web searching, 79% of libraries reported that informal library instruction (at the reference desk or in individual research appointments) included formulating searches for search engines on the open Web. Regarding formal instruction, 62% of all respondents—and 85% of institutions with over 6000 FTEs—reported demonstrating searches on the open Web in classes.

In this survey, only 14% of respondents do not specifically teach students how to formulate Web search statements. Among the librarians who do demonstrate the construction of search statements for the open Web, keyword generation is an important concept (fig. 2). An almost equal percentage teach students how to use synonyms as alternate terms (85%), how to search broader or more narrow terms (86%), and how to mix different combinations of terms (90%). However, only 37% of respondents teach students to vary the order of search terms to manipulate the sequence and relevance of search engine results.

Figure 2. Does library instruction include any of the following strategies to generate keyword terms for use in search engines on the open Web? (Select all that apply)

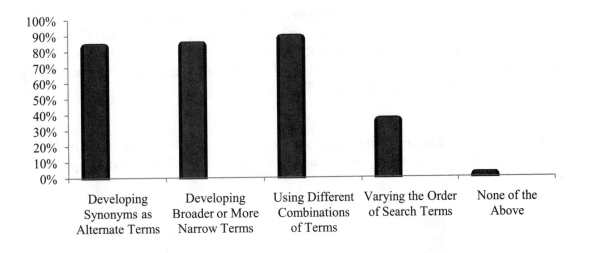

Common techniques that are being applied to instruction on open Web searches include phrase searching (93%), Boolean operators (74%, even though "and" is implied in most popular search engines), and truncation (64%). However, only 48% use symbols such as the plus sign, the minus sign, and the tilde to manipulate Web search results (fig. 3).

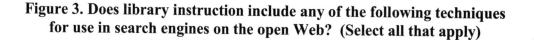

Figure 3. Does library instruction include any of the following techniques for use in search engines on the open Web? (Select all that apply)

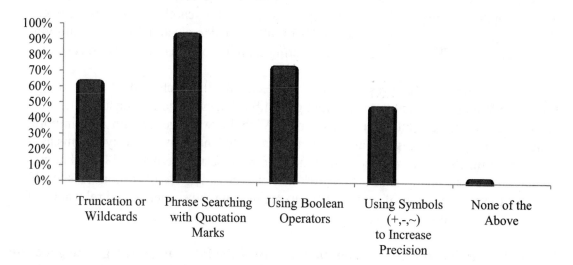

In library databases, command searches are commonly used for field searching, but some respondents also apply this technique in their instruction on the open Web. Site: is the most common type of field parameter, according to this survey, with 47% of respondents reporting that they have included it in Web instruction. Field searching by URL: (37%) is the second most common, followed by searching by Title: (28%) and Link: (24%). Info: (15%) field searches and limiting to Related: sites (14%) were less common techniques. Thirty-four percent of responding librarians do not teach students in any way how to limit searches by field on the open Web (fig. 4).

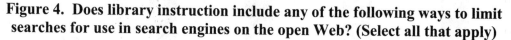

Figure 4. Does library instruction include any of the following ways to limit searches for use in search engines on the open Web? (Select all that apply)

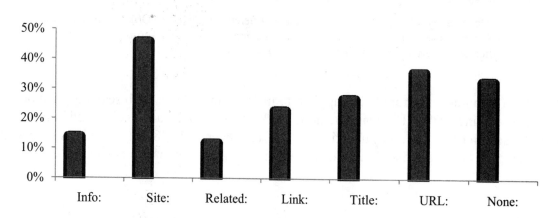

Entry Points to the Web (Questions 15-18)

It is apparent that many libraries have expanded the parameters of academic research when 45% of libraries in this survey reported displaying search boxes or links to search engines on their Web sites. Respondents indicated that they have integrated the following search engines into their library sites:

Alltheweb (by Yahoo)
Alta Vista
Ask.com (aka Ask Jeeves)
Beaucoup
Bing (formerly Live Search & MSN Search)
Clusty (metasearch)
Dogpile (metasearch)
Exalead
Google
Google Book
Google for Government
Google News Archive Search

Google Scholar
Google Uncle Sam
Hakia (semantic)
iTools Search
Ixquick (metasearch)
Looksmart (advertising)
Lycos
Scirus (science)
Search.com (metasearch)
Webcrawler (metasearch)
Yahoo

While some libraries include links to search engines in course and subject guides, others reported that they have placed a search box on their library home page. One institution indicated that they have a campus image that includes a toolbar with search boxes. Two libraries reported including links and evaluative descriptions for search/metasearch engines in a Recommended Search Engines Web page.

Also, 77% percent of respondents integrate directories (collections of Web resources that have been organized into subject categories) into their library materials. The two most popular directories were the Librarians' Internet Index, selected by 46% of libraries and the Internet Public Library, selected by 43% (LII and IPL have since merged into ipl2). Many libraries also point to Infomine (29%) and the WWW Virtual Library (26%). Intute (16%) and the Open Directory Project (13%) are recommended by some libraries as well (fig. 5). Interestingly, all libraries at institutions with 6000 or more FTEs display selected directories on their materials or Web pages.

Figure 5. Do library materials or Web pages point to any subject directories: i.e., collections of Web sites selected and organized for researchers? (Select all that apply)

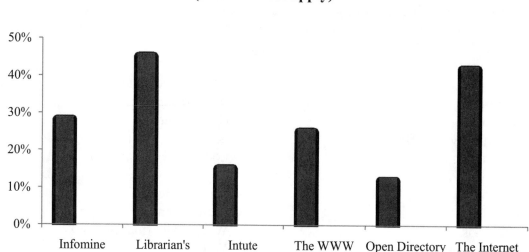

In addition to the directories discussed in the results above, the following general and subject-specific academic directories have been integrated into survey respondents' sites and materials:

AcademicInfo Subject Guides

BUBL Link

Digital Librarian

EuroDocs

FedStats

LANIC: Latin America Network Info Center

My Way

RefSeek directory (beta)

USA.gov

Virtual Learning Resource Center

Virtual Reference Library

Voice of the Shuttle

A number of responding libraries have also developed in-house subject directories for campus research. For example, St. Ambrose University's *Best Info on the Net* link is displayed on other libraries' Web pages. The above results do overlap—libraries were asked to select *all* the directories that apply—but a distinct 36% of respondents do not point to any subject directories in their library materials.

Almost half of the respondents (47%) reported that they teach students to distinguish between subject directories and search engines. Thirty-six percent cover this topic in formal instruction and 39% do so in informal instruction and assistance. This topic isn't typically addressed at 53% of responding libraries. In a related practice, 50% of libraries teach concepts related to the invisible Web (Web sites that are out of reach of search engine crawlers) in formal instruction and 43% do so in informal instruction or assistance.

Other Web Tools (Questions 19-22)

According to this survey, there are a number of open Web tools that have utility for academic research. Seventy-eight percent of responding libraries include a discussion of Google Scholar and Google Books in their formal library instruction, while 74% point to these resources during informal instruction. A mere 11% of libraries are not typically addressing these Google resources in either context.

Forty-six percent of libraries reported that they include discussion of open access journals in their library instruction, while 52% said that this topic is not typically addressed. In response to earlier questions, some libraries commented that they point to *DOAJ: Directory of Open Access Journals* and *Open DOAR: Directory of Open Access Repositories* in their instructional materials.

Social bookmarking is another tool on the open Web that has been used, although more sparingly, by academic libraries (fig. 6). Only 28% of participating libraries reported introducing students to social bookmarking in either formal or informal instruction (but 39% at schools with FTEs over 6000). Of that minority, the most common use of social bookmarking was to share Web sites with other students or faculty (70%). Sixty-seven percent used social bookmarking to store Web sites online rather than on individual workstations. Thirty percent used social bookmarking to locate additional Web sites on a topic and to collect a list of research sites for common use at the reference desk. A mere 12% used this tool to determine the popularity of a Web site by how many times it has been tagged. Several librarians remarked that teaching social bookmarking is an individual endeavor.

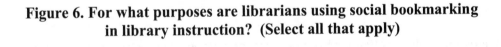

Figure 6. For what purposes are librarians using social bookmarking in library instruction? (Select all that apply)

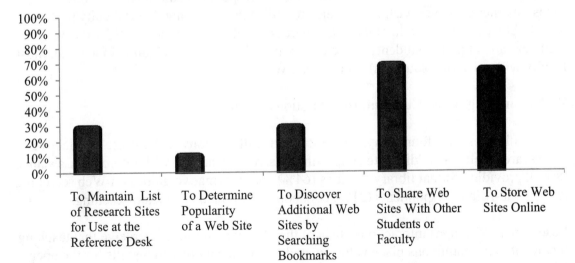

Evaluation and Selection of Web Sites (Questions 23-26)

Fifty percent of respondents now include open Web resources in most library research guides that they prepare for courses or subject areas. An additional 23% reported including Web sites in about half of their guides. Twenty-six percent reported they rarely put open Web resources into research or subject guides. However, 57% of respondents point to sites on the open Web in their library catalogs.

There is near consensus that students' ability to evaluate the Web is an important goal in information literacy instruction. Ninety-three percent of responding libraries include a discussion of evaluating Web content in formal instruction, and 78% evaluate sites in informal instruction/assistance. Librarians reported that they both discuss model Web sites and design evaluative assignments for use in course-related instruction. Faculty either request this instruction from librarians or develop their own criteria for their courses. One librarian qualified her answer by explaining, "We talk in general about evaluation of all resources. Web content is noted but we don't focus narrowly on just that. Format is not as important to us as the fact that users should be looking at all information with a critical eye."

According to this survey, the most popular means of presenting criteria for evaluating open Web content include online tutorials, print handouts, and practice exercises (51%, 53%, and 53% respectively). At schools with 6000 or more FTEs, librarians tend to do less talking about Web evaluation in formal instruction but are more likely to use online tutorials (77%) or print handouts (69%). Libraries of all sizes also reported presenting criteria for evaluating the Web on the library's Web site, in links to material created by other libraries, in course-based handouts and subject guides, and in the course management system.

In the question about evaluating Web content, one respondent submitted the comments, "Most instructors do not wish the students to utilize the Web" and "Our faculty prefer the use of library databases rather than Web sources." Others commented, "Many faculty members do not permit students to use the open Web for research," and "In general, most faculty will not accept sources from the open Web."

Web Searching in the Curriculum (Questions 27-30)

Several libraries have found ways to work with faculty to convey the value of effective Web search skills. In addition to supporting classroom teaching with reference assistance (80%), providing formal library sessions (64%) and informative guides on Web searching (56%), one-fifth of respondents (21%) collaborate with faculty in team-teaching.

Based on their campus interactions, 48% of the librarians surveyed perceive that teaching faculty at their institutions place value on students acquiring research skills for the open Web (fig. 7). Smaller percentages believe that faculty colleagues find Web research skills very valuable (14%) or not valuable (10%). Almost a third of respondents (28%) have no opinion or don't know to what degree faculty value Web research skills.

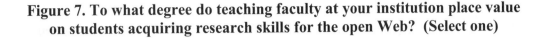

Figure 7. To what degree do teaching faculty at your institution place value on students acquiring research skills for the open Web? (Select one)

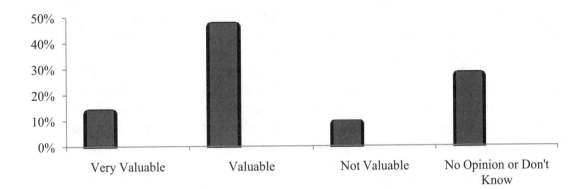

Librarians are being proactive—using faculty development, publicity, collaborative teaching and informal conversations—to get faculty to recognize the potential of using the open Web for academic research. In fact, when librarians were asked how they promote themselves as colleagues who provide instruction on open Web research, 85% responded that they use informal interactions to market their services. At one institution, librarians intentionally attend department meetings and maintain membership on curriculum committees. Sixty percent allow the demonstration of Web-based research to speak for itself. One respondent noted that presentations at faculty meetings and orientation fairs have helped to spread the word. Another reported, "We're offering well-attended workshops on advanced Google and Google Books/Scholar to faculty and staff." Fifty percent of respondents reported promoting their services on the library Web page or in print materials. Forty-five percent are using e-mails to market some aspect of Web search instruction. Fifteen percent of respondents do not actively promote library instruction on open Web searching. However, one respondent in this category reported, "It's not specifically promoted but available when needed for particular assignments."

When information literacy programs are integrated into the curriculum, one way to demonstrate the value of teaching Web search strategies is to include those skills in written assessment tools. However, 49% of the libraries that responded to this survey do not include Web search skills in assessment measures. In fact, six respondents specifically commented that their libraries do not yet have written assessment tools, although some said they are "working on that." Of the libraries that are including Web search skills in assessment, equal percentages are doing so with student competency standards, with pre-tests and post-tests (including a proficiency exam), and with evaluation rubrics for assignments. Half of the schools with FTEs over 4000 have student competency standards or learning goals, but written assessment is less common at the smaller schools.

Conclusion

Analysis of student bibliographies and faculty observation suggests that undergraduates rely on commercial search engines as much as or more than library-based resources. Considering the centrality of the Web in student research behavior, it isn't surprising that nearly all responding libraries provide some instruction on searching the Web. In truth, this task is driven not by student behavior alone but also by the academic library's recognition of the growing scope of information. In the past, librarians oriented students to the various facets of a collection: books, scholarly articles, reference materials, databases. Increasingly, reliable information is found outside the walls of the library. Many librarians are now introducing students to the realm of legitimate online information, including online repositories, digital collections, open access scholarship sites, government information sites, online directories, and specialized pathfinders.

The survey reveals that libraries deliver Web instruction in a variety of formats. Traditional demonstrations and hands-on practice are useful to reach a number of students, and most libraries do appear to have a facility for hands-on instruction. The results indicate that librarians believe in the value of course-specific instruction. On the other hand, the high rate of one-on-one assistance suggests that individual instruction continues to respond to the diversity of information needs that students bring to the library. Likewise, although online tutorials are very well suited to students' penchant for self-mediated formats, this survey demonstrates that many undergraduates still seek face-to-face help.

The results above indicate that while the vast majority of librarians provide instruction on the open Web, some libraries do not specifically teach students how to formulate search statements. The presumption is that the algorithm of popular search engines will find useful information, regardless of the effectiveness of the search statement. Unfortunately, left to the approach that they use for recreational Web surfing, students often construct very simplistic search statements that lead to less relevant results. For purposes of effective academic research, it can be empowering for students to know a few strategies that capitalize on the search mechanisms of commercial engines.

Due to the variability of search functions in popular search engines, the literature advocates teaching the general concepts of Web searching rather than giving students tactics for specific search engines. Also, as revealed in the discussion above, many Web search concepts can be reinforced by techniques that apply to online library databases. When it comes to the Web, an additional skill to convey to students is to consult the documentation available for their favorite search engine.

According to this survey, many libraries now place an Internet search box on their library home page. Of course, all search engines (and their results) differ due to their individual relevancy ranking algorithms. Libraries either have to determine which search engine(s) best serves their students or display a selection of search tools for students to choose from.

Likewise, a selection process must be applied to include Web directories on the library site or in course-related materials. Pointing to an excellent subject directory can compensate for students' unsophisticated search skills by guiding them to quality Web sites. Although the level of selectivity may vary among directories, the fact that sites have been reviewed by human beings (not generated by automated search engines) generally leads to higher quality and greater relevance.

Unfortunately, directories are typically confused with digital libraries, databases, online reference collections or search engines. This confusion may come from the search feature that is available in some directories, but the distinction is that, unlike these other resources, directories are simply collections of selected Web links.

Subject directories are one of the most effective means to get at information in the invisible (or deep) Web. The inaccessibility of this portion of the Web makes it difficult to locate the information in governmental databases, academic resource guides, digital collections, and other resources that aren't indexed. It isn't necessary for undergraduates to know how search engine spiders crawl through the Web and create the keyword indexes that are subsequently searched. However, students will be better information users if they merely understand that significant content exists beyond the results of conventional search engines.

When libraries rely on open Web tools for research, the breadth of instruction will change. For example, librarians are now teaching students to recognize the complexities of Google Scholar. Although Google Scholar can be a valuable discovery tool for peer-reviewed articles, theses, preprints and even conference proceedings, it can be difficult to discern the derivation of items. Librarians can help students differentiate the variety of origins and formats of Google Scholar's materials. Also, because Google Scholar does not uniformly provide full text, students will require instruction in library-funded databases to locate the articles that they encounter in Google Scholar's citations. Google Books, on the other hand, *can* expand libraries' e-book collections, particularly when it provides full-text versions of books in the public domain. Librarians will be instrumental in leading novice researchers to be aware of these outside resources.

Open access journals have also begun to have an impact on the way that librarians guide students to resources. Various portals, including scholarly repositories and online journals, allow researchers to locate scholarly articles on the open Web. While open access publications are free of the financial and legal barriers of conventional publishing models, they are, unfortunately, beyond the scope of many library indexes. Libraries will have to determine how to best teach undergraduates to locate articles in open access collections.

One of the most important responsibilities of the academic librarian is to help undergraduates locate authoritative information. It is evident in the literature that it is a common practice to place recommended Web links on research guides or course management systems for individual classes. The response to this practice is mixed. On one hand, pointing to the best sites is a means for librarians to model quality Web resources. On the other hand, if students are consistently supplied with a collection of resources, they lose the opportunity to learn to search and evaluate Web sites for themselves. Fortunately, many librarians reported that they choose to annotate the sites that they point to; carefully written annotations can demonstrate the qualities to look for in Web resources.

With the increasing numbers of high-quality digital collections, archives, and repositories, academic libraries will have to address how to organize recommended sites for reference and student use. Social bookmarking may be a valuable tool in this endeavor. It enables Internet users to bookmark favorite Web sites, tag those sites by subject and share them with others. If bookmarks are made public, users can also see how many other people have pointed to a particular site. One respondent commented that she capitalizes on the networking capability of social bookmarking, using it for "collaborative research and learning." Additionally, a creative application of a popular social bookmarking site appears in the collection of submitted documents in this *CLIP Note*: the library at Salisbury University has tagged a number of Web sites in their Delicious account and embedded the tags into library subject guides. This allows students to click in to Web resources that have been selected by the library.

While open Web resources hold promise for undergraduate researchers, librarians are aware that sometimes faculty limit use of the Internet for coursework. Some instructors are not satisfied with the Web as the sole source of information or express their preference for subscription databases and other traditional library sources. As the open Web continues to be a pervasive source of information, team teaching with faculty can provide a shared venue for librarians to teach students to be more intentional in their search and evaluation strategies.

Like most library services, information literacy instruction supports the mission of the campus-wide curriculum. In this light, it is not surprising that the factor that appears to have the strongest correlation with librarians engaging the open Web is the extent to which they perceive that Web research skills have value in their academic communities. When librarians perceive that colleagues place value on this facet of information literacy, they embody a strong commitment to equipping students to be effective Web researchers.

At institutions where librarians selected *very valuable* in response to the question, "To what degree do teaching faculty at your institution place value on students acquiring research skills for the open Web?" there are considerably higher percentages of frequency of instruction, including course-related instruction, in all formats and contexts. That instruction includes formatting searches for the open Web as well as the inclusion of subject directories, open access journals, social bookmarking, and Google Scholar as topics of instruction. Web searching is also more likely to be assessed in written assessment tools at these institutions.

The practices of the academic libraries in this survey demonstrate that there is significant attention given to teaching students how to effectively search and evaluate the Web, both in formal and individual instruction. However, there is more work to be done, particularly at smaller institutions, to teach students how to access Web resources of the highest academic quality. As usual, librarians will encourage one another in this endeavor, as evidenced by the generous sharing of documents that follow.

SELECTED BIBLIOGRAPHY

Arnold, J. M. and E. A. Jayne. 1998. Dangling by a Slender Thread: The Lessons and Implications of Teaching the World Wide Web to Freshmen. *Journal of Academic Librarianship* 24 (1): 43-52.

Boening, C. H. and D. J. Grimes. 2001. Worries with the Web: A Look at Student Use of Web Resources. *College and Research Libraries* 62 (1): 11-23.

Cason, C. and A. M. van Scoyoc. 2006. The Electronic Academic Library: Undergraduate Research Behavior in a Library Without Books. *portal: Libraries and the Academy* 6 (1): 47-58.

Cohen, L. B. 2007. A Query-Based Approach in Web Search Instruction: An Assessment of Current Practice. *Research Strategies* 20: 442-457.

Colaric, S. M. 2003. Instruction for Web Searching: An Empirical Study. *College and Research Libraries* 64 (2): 111-122.

Davis, P. M. 2003. Effect of the Web on Undergraduate Citation Behavior: Guiding Student Scholarship in a Networked Age. *portal: Libraries and the Academy* 3 (1): 41-51.

Devine, J. and F. Egger-Sider. 2005. Google, the Invisible Web, and Librarians: Slaying the Research Goliath. *Internet Reference Services Quarterly* 10 (3/4): 89-101.

Diaz, K. R., S. Monoi, and N. O'Hanlon. 2005. Online Searching Skills: Development of an Inventory to Assess Self-Efficacy. *Journal of Academic Librarianship* 31 (2): 98-105.

Eisenberg, M. B. and A. J. Head. 2009. Lessons Learned: How College Students Seek Information in the Digital Age. *Project Information Literacy Report.* http://projectinfolit.org/pdfs/PIL_Fall2009_Year1Report_12_2009.pdf. (accessed April 5, 2010).

Ettinger, D. 2007. The Triumph of Expediency: The Impact of Google Scholar on Library Instruction. *Journal of Library Administration* 46 (3/4): 65-72.

Fonseca, T. and M. King. 2000. Incorporating the Internet into Traditional Library Instruction. *Computers in Libraries* 20 (2): 38-42.

Hartman, K. A. and L. B. Mullen. 2006. Google Scholar and the Library Web Site: The Early Response by ARL Libraries. *College and Research Libraries* 67 (2): 106-122.

Herring, S. D. 2001. Faculty Acceptance of the World Wide Web for Student Research. *College and Research Libraries* 62, no. 3: 251-258.

Hricko, M. 2002. Using the Invisible Web to Teach Information Literacy. *Journal of Library Administration* 37 (3/4): 379-386.

Jones, S. and M. Madden. 2002. The Internet Goes to College: How Students Are Living in the Future with Today's Technology. *Pew Internet and American Life Project*. http://www.authoring.pewinternet.org/Reports/2002/The-Internet-Goes-to-College.aspx. (accessed: February 4, 2010).

Martin, P. 2006. Google as Teacher: Everything Your Students Know They Learned From Searching Google. *College and Research Libraries News* 67 (2): 100-101.

Martzoukou, K. 2008. Students' Attitudes Towards Web Search Engines—Increasing Appreciation of Sophisticated Search Strategies. *Libri* 58: 182-201.

OCLC (Online Computer Library Center, Inc.). 2002. OCLC White Paper on the Information Habits of College Students: How Academic Librarians Can Influence Students' Web-Based Information Choices. http://www5.oclc.org/downloads/community/informationhabits.pdf (accessed: February 4, 2010).

Thompson, C. 2003. Information Illiterate of Lazy: How College Students Use the Web for Research. *portal: Libraries and the Academy* 3 (2): 259-268.

Tolppanen, B. P. 1999. A Survey of World Wide Web Use by Freshman English Students: Results and Implications for Bibliographic Instruction. *Internet Reference Services Quarterly* 4 (4): 43-53.

Tomaiuolo, N. G. 2005. Faculty Views of Open Web Resource Use by College Students. *The Journal of Academic Librarianship* 31(5): 559-566.

Wright, C. A. 2004. The Academic Library as a Gateway to the Internet: An Analysis of the Extent and Nature of Search Engine Access from Academic Library Home Pages. *College and Research Libraries* 65 (4): 276-286.

York, M. C. 2005. Calling the Scholars Home: Google Scholar as a Tool for Rediscovering the Academic Library. *Internet Reference Services Quarterly* 10 (3/4): 117-133.

CLIP Note SURVEY RESULTS

***CLIP Note* Survey: Web Research in Library Instruction**

The following questions are designed to gather information regarding how libraries have integrated Web search strategies into their information literacy instruction. In response to questions that ask about general practice, do your best to represent the library instruction that you have observed in your department.

This CLIP Note will compile instructional materials to model how libraries are teaching Web searching skills. Please supplement your survey response with sample documents including the following:

+Online tutorials or print handouts related to Web searching
+Class activities or practice exercises
+Pathfinders to recommended Web search tools
+Criteria for evaluating Web sites
+Information literacy objectives or assessment tools that include Web search skills

*Please note that the survey will ask for FTE information for faculty, students, librarians and library staff, and number of library volumes. You may wish to compile this information before you begin.

1. Institution Name

2. Address

3. Name of Respondent

4. Title

5. Work telephone number

6. Fax number

7. E-mail address

8. On average, how often do librarians at your institution provide instruction or assistance—either formal or informal—on searching the open Web? (Select approximate answer)

44.8% (52) ONE OR MORE TIMES DAILY
21.6% (25) SEVERAL TIMES A WEEK
19.8% (23) ONCE EVERY WEEK OR TWO

8.6% (10) ONCE A MONTH
5.2% (6) RARELY OR NOT AT ALL

2 respondents skipped question

9. What formats, if any, do librarians use for instruction on searching the open Web? (Select all that apply)

79.3% (92) DEMONSTRATIONS
66.4% (77) HANDS-ON PRACTICE
90.5% (105) ONE-ON-ONE ASSISTANCE
34.5% (40) ONLINE TUTORIALS
30.2% (35) PRINT MATERIALS
2.6% (3) NONE
11.2% (13) OTHER (please specify) _____

2 respondents skipped question

10. In what formal contexts, if any, does instruction on searching the open Web take place? (Select all that apply)

27.8% (32) LIBRARY ORIENTATION
52.2% (60) INSTRUCTION IN THE FIRST-YEAR PROGRAM
83.5% (96) COURSE-RELATED LIBRARY INSTRUCTION
40.0% (46) INSTRUCTION FOR SENIOR THESES OR PROJECTS
18.3% (21) REQUIRED OR ELECTIVE CREDIT-BEARING LIBRARY COURSES
6.1% (7) NONE
16.5% (19) OTHER (please specify) _____

3 respondents skipped question

11. Does library instruction include formulating searches for search engines on the open Web? (Select all that apply)

61.7% (71) YES, FORMAL LIBRARY INSTRUCTION
79.1% (91) YES, INFORMAL LIBRARY INSTRUCTION
        including assistance at the Reference Desk and individual research appointments
13.9% (16) NO, THIS IS NOT TYPICALLY ADDRESSED (Skips to #11)

3 respondents skipped question

12. Does library instruction include any of the following strategies to generate keyword terms for use in search engines on the open Web? (Select all that apply)

84.8% (84) DEVELOPING SYNONYMS AS ALTERNATE TERMS
85.9% (85) DEVELOPING BROADER OR MORE NARROW TERMS
89.9% (89) USING DIFFERENT COMBINATIONS OF TERMS
37.4% (37) VARYING THE ORDER OF SEARCH TERMS
3.0% (3) NONE OF THE ABOVE

19 respondents skipped question

13. Does library instruction include any of the following techniques for use in search engines on the open Web? (Select all that apply)

63.6% (63) TRUNCATION OR WILDCARDS
93.9% (93) PHRASE SEARCHING WITH QUOTATION MARKS
73.7% (73) USING BOOLEAN OPERATORS
48.5% (48) USING SYMBOLS (PLUS SIGN, MINUS SIGN, TILDE) TO
            INCREASE PRECISION
3.0% (3) NONE OF THE ABOVE

19 respondents skipped question

14. Does library instruction include any of the following ways to limit searches for use in search engines on the open Web? (Select all that apply)

14.6% (14) INFO:
46.9% (45) SITE:
13.5% (13) RELATED:
24.0% (23) LINK:
28.1% (27) TITLE:
37.5% (36) URL:
34.4% (33) NONE OF THE ABOVE

22 respondents skipped question

15. Does your library Web site display search boxes or links to specific search engines on the open Web?

54.9% (62) NO
45.1% (51) YES (Please specify) _____

5 respondents skipped question

16. Do library materials or Web pages point to any subject directories; i.e., collections of Web sites selected and organized for researchers? (Select all that apply)

29.0% (29) INFOMINE
46.0% (46) LIBRARIAN'S INTERNET INDEX
16.0% (16) INTUTE
26.0% (26) THE WWW VIRTUAL LIBRARY
13.0% (13) OPEN DIRECTORY PROJECT
43.0% (43) THE INTERNET PUBLIC LIBRARY
23.0% (23) LIBRARY MATERIALS DO NOT POINT TO SUBJECT DIRECTORIES
36.0% (36) OTHER (Please specify)

18 respondents skipped question

17. Does library instruction distinguish between subject directories and search engines? (Select all that apply)

36.0% (41) YES, FORMAL LIBRARY INSTRUCTION
38.6% (44) YES, INFORMAL LIBRARY INSTRUCTION
        including assistance at the Reference Desk and individual research appointments
53.5% (61) NO, THIS IS NOT TYPICALLY ADDRESSED

4 respondents skipped question

18. Does library instruction address the concept of the invisible Web or deep Web; i.e., sites beyond the reach of search engine crawlers? (Select all that apply)

49.6% (56) YES, FORMAL LIBRARY INSTRUCTION
43.4% (49) YES, INFORMAL LIBRARY INSTRUCTION
        including assistance at the Reference Desk and individual research appointments
40.7% (46) NO

5 respondents skipped question

19. Does library instruction include discussion *of* Google Scholar or Google Books? (Select all that apply)

77.9% (88) YES, FORMAL LIBRARY INSTRUCTION
74.3% (84) YES, INFORMAL LIBRARY INSTRUCTION
        including assistance at the Reference Desk and individual research appointments
10.6% (12) NO, THIS IS NOT TYPICALLY ADDRESSED

5 respondents skipped question

20. Does library instruction include discussion of open access scholarship repositories; e.g. Public Library of Science, Open Humanities Press, or others? (Select all that apply)

33.6% (38) YES, FORMAL LIBRARY INSTRUCTION
39.8% (45) YES, INFORMAL LIBRARY INSTRUCTION
            including assistance at the Reference Desk and individual research appointments
52.2% (59) NO, THIS IS NOT TYPICALLY ADDRESSED

5 respondents skipped question

21. Does library instruction include discussion of social bookmarking?
(Select all that apply)

20.4% (23) YES, FORMAL LIBRARY INSTRUCTION
23.9% (27) YES, INFORMAL LIBRARY INSTRUCTION
            including assistance at the Reference Desk and individual research appointments
70.8% (80) NO, THIS IS NOT TYPICALLY ADDRESSED (Skips to #23)

5 respondents skipped question

22. For what purposes are librarians using social bookmarking in library instruction?
(Select all that apply)

66.7% (22) TO STORE WEB SITES ONLINE
69.7% (23) TO SHARE WEB SITES WITH OTHER STUDENTS OR FACULTY
30.3% (10) TO DISCOVER ADDITIONAL WEB SITES BY SEARCHING
            BOOKMARKS
12.1% (4) TO DETERMINE THE POPULARITY OF A WEB SITE
30.3% (10) TO MAINTAIN A LIST OF RESEARCH SITES FOR USE AT THE
            REFERENCE DESK
18.2% (6) OTHER (Please specify)

85 respondents skipped question

23. How often do library research guides, prepared for courses or subject areas, include open Web resources?

49.6% (56) OFTEN (at least 3/4 of the time)
23.0% (26) SOMETIMES (1/2 of the time)
25.7% (29) RARELY (1/4 of the time)
1.8% (2) NEVER

5 respondents skipped question

24. Does the online library catalog point to sites on the open Web (other than fee-based resources)?

57.5% (65) YES
42.5% (48) NO

5 respondents skipped question

25. Does library instruction include discussion of evaluating Web content for objectivity, currency, or credibility? (Select all that apply)

92.9% (104) YES, FORMAL LIBRARY INSTRUCTION
77.7% (87) YES, INFORMAL LIBRARY INSTRUCTION
          including assistance at the Reference Desk and individual research appointments
3.6% (4) NO, THIS IS NOT TYPICALLY ADDRESSED

6 respondents skipped question

26. Does your library present criteria for evaluating Web content? (Select all that apply)

50.9% (58) YES, IN ONLINE TUTORIALS
52.6% (60) YES, IN PRINT MATERIALS
53.5% (61) YES, WITH PRACTICE EXERCISES
7.9% (9) NO, EVALUATION CRITERIA ARE NOT PRESENTED
26.3% (30) OTHER (please specify) _____

4 respondents skipped question

27. To what degree do teaching faculty at your institution place value on students acquiring research skills for the open Web? (Select one)

14.2% (16) VERY VALUABLE
47.8% (54) VALUABLE
9.7% (11) NOT VALUABLE
28.3% (32) NO OPINION / DON'T KNOW

5 respondents skipped question

28. In what ways, if any, do librarians collaborate with faculty to promote effective Web search skills in research related to coursework? (Select all that apply)

21.2% (24) IN THE FORM OF TEAM TEACHING
64.6% (73) BY PROVIDING FORMAL LIBRARY INSTRUCTION ON WEB
SEARCHING
80.5% (91) BY SUPPORTING CLASSROOM TEACHING WITH REFERENCE
SERVICES
55.8% (63) BY PROVIDING INFORMATION ON WEB SEARCH SKILLS, IN PRINT
OR ONLINE
8.8% (10) THERE IS NO LIBRARIAN-FACULTY COLLABORATION ON
PROMOTING WEB SEARCH SKILLS
8.0% (9) OTHER (please specify)

5 respondents skipped question

29. How do librarians market themselves as colleagues who can teach Web-based research as well as traditional library instruction? (Select all that apply)

49.6% (56) ON THE LIBRARY WEB PAGE OR IN PRINT MATERIALS
85.0% (96) IN INFORMAL INTERACTIONS OR BY WORD OF MOUTH
45.1% (51) BY E-MAIL ANNOUNCEMENTS
60.2% (68) BY DEMONSTRATIONS OF WEB-BASED RESEARCH IN LIBRARY
INSTRUCTION
15.0% (17) LIBRARY INSTRUCTION ON OPEN WEB SEARCHING IS NOT
PROMOTED
8.0% (9) OTHER (please specify)

5 respondents skipped question

30. How does the library include Web search skills in its written assessment tools? (Select all that apply)

25.7% (28) IN STUDENT COMPETENCY STANDARDS OR LEARNING GOALS
25.7% (28) IN PRE-TESTS OR POST-TESTS ON INFORMATION LITERACY
23.9% (26) IN EVALUATION RUBRICS FOR ASSIGNMENTS OR ACTIVITIES
48.6 (53) WEB SEARCH SKILLS ARE NOT INCLUDED IN CURRENT
ASSESSMENT
TOOLS
8.3% (9) OTHER (please specify)

9 respondents skipped question

31. Where do librarians provide hands-on online instruction? (Select all that apply)

98.2% (112) IN A LIBRARY BUILDING
64.9% (74) IN ANOTHER CAMPUS BUILDING
41.2% (47) USING LAPTOPS IN A WIRELESS ENVIRONMENT
1.8% (2) LIBRARIANS DO NOT HAVE ACCESS TO A COMPUTER FACILITY
        FOR HANDS-ON INSTRUCTION
0.9% (1) LIBRARIANS DO NOT CHOOSE TO USE HANDS-ON INSTRUCTION

4 respondents skipped question

32. Which of the following best describes your library's position as a campus organization? (Select one)

57.9% (66) OPERATES AS AN INDEPENDENT UNIT
28.1% (32) OPERATES INDEPENDENTLY BUT IS PART OF A LARGER UNIT
9.6% (11) MERGED WITH INFORMATION TECHNOLOGY
4.4% (5) OTHER (please specify) _____

4 respondents skipped question

33. Carnegie Classification of Institution (Select one)

23.4% (26) Master's M: Master's Colleges and Universities (medium programs)
35.1% (39) Master's S: Master's Colleges and Universities (small programs)
30.6% (34) Bac / A&S: Baccalaureate Colleges – Arts & Sciences
9.0% (10) Bac / Diverse: Baccalaureate Colleges – Diverse Fields
1.8% (2) Bac / Assoc: Baccalaureate / Associate's Colleges

7 respondents skipped question

34. Type of Institution

25.4% (29) PUBLIC
74.6% (85) PRIVATE

4 respondents skipped question

35. FTE Students: lowest = 589   highest = 15,000
6 respondents skipped question

36. FTE Faculty: lowest = 43   highest = 1227
9 respondents skipped question

37. FTE Librarians: lowest = 2   highest = 29
6 respondents skipped question

38. FTE Library Support Staff: lowest = 1   highest = 40
7 respondents skipped question

39. Number of Library Volumes: lowest = 60,000   highest = 3,500,000
7 respondents skipped question

40. Please submit sample documents including the following:

+Online tutorials or print handouts related to Web searching
+Class activities or practice exercises
+Pathfinders to recommended Web search tools
+Criteria for evaluating Web sites
+Information literacy objectives or assessment tools that include Web search skills

41. I give permission to publish any document I send with this completed survey in a *CLIP Note* publication

The following copyright statement is required to publish any document I send with a completed survey in a *CLIP Note* publication:

DOCUMENTS:

Defining the Nature of the Web

WEB SEARCHING BASICS

Searching for information on the World Wide Web can be both easy and difficult at the same time. A basic understanding of what the Web can and can not do will be helpful in deciding where and how to search. The huge amount of information available, one major reason the Web is so attractive, is also one of its major drawbacks. How do you find the one piece of information that will meet your specific need out of thousands or millions of sites? And how do you know that the information you find is valid? Like any skill, searching the Web takes practice to be efficient and effective.

When considering using a Web search for a particular information need, keep the following things in mind:

- **The Kind of Information Available**
Government agency information, current news, consumer information, popular culture and entertainment, **non-proprietary research** in science and technology, information from political, cultural, and religious organizations and educational papers and reports.

- **The Nature of the Web**
It is a relatively inexpensive way to distribute information; it is immediate, anyone with an internet connection and a browser can "publish" on the Web; there is no review of the contents by experts or scholars in the field, there are no rules and regulations regarding the content and structure of sites and it can change daily, even hourly. Because of these characteristics the end-user can not assume that the information found is accurate and authoritative. Each web source has to be evaluated for accuracy, authoritativeness, and currency.

Finally a choice must be made as to which type of search mechanism to use. There are two major types of search tools available, **subject directories** and **search engines**. Although the line between the two is becoming increasingly blurred as they grow in sophistication, the lack of human input into the search result with Search Engines and the limitation to searching only by fairly broad categories with Subject Directories necessitates some critical thinking about the type of information needed.

- **Subject directories** are collections of Web sites organized by human indexers into subject trees. You can browse down through the subject subdivisions to more and more specific topics or search by keywords that index the words that appear in the Web page titles or at best short descriptive annotations of the content. They are a good place to start if you are not sure of exactly what your focus will be. They cover only a small percentage of available sites, but have a high percentage of good sites because of the human filtering element.
For academic information needs the best Subject Directory available is **Infomine** at **<http://infomine.ucr.edu>**

- **Search Engines**  are computer-generated indexes of **all** the words on a Web page. Searching is by keywords, i.e. does the search term appear **any where** in the text of the page? The better search engines cover 60% to 80% of all Web sites, but with no human evaluation of content, results can be confusing. Also, recent studies have shown a low percentage of overlap from one search engine to another. **No Search Engine is able to index the entire Internet.**

The list of returned sites is usually returned sorted according to "relevancy," which means the more the search term appears on the Web page or the closer the term appears to the beginning of the Web page, the higher its relevancy score. To restrict the search to the exact phrase when there are two or more search terms, use quotation marks as explained below.

In addition to Google you could try your search in one of the other search engines such as:

AllTheWeb.com <www.alltheweb.com>

Ask (formerly Ask Jeeves)< www.ask.com>

Clusty < www.clusty.com>

Dogpile <www.dogpile.com>

Metacrawler <www.metacrawler.com>

The last two of these are what is known as "Meta-Search Engines" because they run the search in more than one of the standard search engines at one time. The drawback to this strategy is that the order of the search engines chosen by default may not be the best choice for a particular information need. Also the searches are not run concurrently and some search engines time out before

the particular search is run. These problems have been addressed by a new generation of meta-searchers such as **Browsys.**

< www.browsys.com/finder/index.php >. Here you type in your search terms, click on the type of web resource you think would be best and run the search in the various search engines available by clicking on the button for that specific engine. This makes it a quick and easy way to compare results of different search engines.

If a useable site is not retrieved in the first 20 sites displayed, you probably need to try searching another search engine or try different search terms.

Search Tips: It is strongly recommended that you review the help screen of each directory or search engine used. They explain the various methods that can be used to tailor your search to retrieve a higher percentage of good hits. Some general hints that may prove helpful are the following:

The Boolean search operators AND, OR and NOT allow you to focus your search results to results closer to your information needs. **AND** between two words tells the computer that both terms will need to be in an item for it to be retrieved. **OR** between two words tells the computer to retrieve items that have either of the two words. **NOT** or the hyphen character **-** is used to exclude ANY article that contains that word that follows it, even if the other search terms appear at the site. Most of the search engines listed above automatically use the AND operator between search terms.

When searching for a phrase, use quotation marks. For instance "home schooling" will only return sites that have those words in that exact order. Without the quotation marks, sites that have the word schooling in one section and home in another would also be retrieved.

When searching for a site on a particular individual or company or organization, it is a good idea to use proper capitalization. <Apple> will retrieve sites that mention Apple Computers while <apple> will retrieve those sites plus any that mention the fruit.

If after following all these tips, you still are not turning up the information you need, do not hesitate to ask a reference librarian for help.

LIBRARIES, MEDIA SERVICES, & ARCHIVES

ST. CATHERINE UNIVERSITY

Library Home   Hours   Contact Us   Search our Site

⌄ Books, Articles & More   ⌄ Help with Research   ⌄ Library Services   ⌄ About the Library

Search CLICnet: [   ] in: [Books and more ▼] (Go)   [Quick Links... ▼] (Go)

Help with Research

Subject Research Guides

Database Guides

Research Tools and Tutorials

Access and Technology Help

RefWorks

Guides for Citing

Core Curriculum: TRW & GSJ

Finding Websites

The World Wide Web is a terrific resource for finding information on some topics, but may be inappropriate for others. When you have an assignment, be sure to ask your professor what types of resources you may use. This page will discuss the information you can and can't get on the Web, and offer some tips for searching and navigating. Other Library pages offer links to Internet search engines and advice on evaluating the information you find on the Web.

- Why use the World Wide Web?
- What you (usually) can't find on the Web
- Top ways to find relevant Web sites
- Hints and tips for searching the Web
- Just for fun

The Web is one of the favorite Internet services used by people today. Some of its many features include long-distance communication, remote searching, hyperlinked pages, and the availability of music, pictures, video, and text documents. It is especially helpful in finding:

- Information provided by state, federal and international government
- Facts, statistics, reports, studies and other educational works
- News, current events and press releases
- Information on organizations, educational institutions, and companies
- Selected electronic journals, texts and books out of copyright
- Reference works, such as encyclopedias, directories and dictionaries

Unlike a library, where the resources are carefully selected for quality and organized by subject, the Web makes available a variety of information sources. ***The quality of these sources will vary widely.*** It is your responsibility as a student and researcher to determine if the Web is a good place to find information on a topic, or to assess the quality of a particular Web source. Read more about evaluating Web sources below.

What you (usually) can't find on the Web

Periodical articles

Using the Web, you can frequently find current news stories and a few scholarly articles. Generally speaking, the majority of articles published in newspapers, journals and magazines are **not** available to the average Web user. Sure, you may find references to these items and even complete citations, but unless you are using an index or database to which the St. Kate's Library subscribes, you will usually not find the full text of these articles. The Library pays yearly fees to access journal articles for use by our students, faculty and staff.

Books

Generally speaking, you will not find the full text of books on the Web. Yes, Google Book Search allows you to retrieve many books that can be read or downloaded. Most of these books are older and out of copyright, while some of them have been published on the Web with the permission of the publisher. These are exceptions rather than rules. Most of the books found by way of Google Book Search must be ordered (from a publisher or bookseller) or borrowed from a library.

The St. Kate's Library does "own" many books that are available online to our community, again, on a subscription basis. You can identify these books using CLICnet, the online catalogs of the ACTC private college consortium. (Read more about e-books.)

Top Ways to Locate Relevant Web sites

- Use a search engine such as Google or Yahoo. Learn how to enter searches most effectively and how to use the advanced search features to filter out unwanted results.
- Use a subject index or directory
- Visit the Blackboard site for your course and check the syllabus or "External Links" area for sites recommended by your professor.
- Visit the homepage of your department. They may list good sites for your field.
- Visit the subject guides on the Library's Web site. Librarians search and collect sites that our students may find useful.

- Visit the homepage of a professional or research organization that ties to your topic. They may link to research findings, publications or other Web sites on the topic.
- Follow the links from one reputable Web site to another. Look for language such as "Resources" or "Research."
- Look for Web sites in the text or on the reference lists of journal articles. Authors often include the URLs of Web sites they use.

Hints and Tips for Searching the Web

By improving your skills as a Web searcher, you will increase the likelihood of finding relevant information -- and save yourself a lot of the time it takes to shift through unwanted, commercially-oriented pages. Get more help:

- Searching using Boolean operators
- Choosing search terms

How are your Web searching skills?
Take a quiz and find out!
Links to the answers are at the bottom of each quiz.
Even experts can learn new skills!

How to evaluate the Web sites you have found

Found some Web pages that look good? Great!! Your job as a scholar is only partially done, though, since you now now need to carefully select those that you will use in your paper.

Unlike journal articles and books that go through an editorial process and possibly peer review, just about anyone with a computer can publish a Web site. Read now about how to evaluate and select the Web pages you will use.

Just for fun....

What have you learned about evaluative criteria that you can apply to the pages linked below?

Would *you* use any of them as sources in a paper? Why or why not?

- Feline Reactions to Bearded Men -->
- More from the Annals of Improbable Research
- Mankato, Minnesota, vacation Mecca of the Midwest
- WhiteHouse.org (not to be confused with WhiteHouse.gov)
- Dihydrogen Monoxide in the Dairy Industry
- California's Velcro Crop Under Challenge
- *The Onion*: America's Finest News Source
- The Jackalope Conspiracy

DiMenna-Nyselius Library

Research Assistance

Databases vs. Websites

What's the difference between databases and websites?

Databases	Websites
• Fee-based. The library **pays** for you to have access to them	• Mostly **free**
• Available only to members of the **Fairfield community**	• Available to **anyone**
• Provide **value-added information** that has been selected, edited, and reviewed by experts • **"Peer-reviewed"** scholarly articles	• Provide information that may be **unfiltered, unedited, and created by anyone** • Articles probably do not go through a review process
• **Updated** regularly	• May **not be updated**
• **Trustworthy, reliable**	• **Not necessarily** trustworthy or reliable
• Purpose is to **advance knowledge**	• Purpose may be to **sell you something or sway your opinion**
• **Use for scholarly research, but remember, even scholarly sources can have a bias!**	• **Use with caution for scholarly research; remember to evaluate the source!**

Internet and Web-based Databases

Carol Grotnes Belk Library | Campus Box 2550, Elon, NC 27244 | © Elon University

Frequently, instructors will specify that you not use Internet resources when researching papers or presentations. There are, *however*, many Web-based databases that are available via the Internet that are not considered "Internet resources." Internet resources and Web-based databases have some distinguishing characteristics that will help you to recognize them. **Very few magazines, newspapers, and journals are found full-text on the Internet via commercial search engines like *Yahoo, Alta Vista, Infoseek*, etc.**

	Internet	Web-based Databases
Cost	Free	Subscription Costs (*free to students through library*)
Access	Available from any computer with Internet access.	Only available from networked computers ON CAMPUS, or with a password
Articles written by	Anyone – the Internet is open to all - and there is no guarantee that the parson named on the page is the one responsible for the content.	Journalists Reporters Professionals within a field Scholars
Content	Anything, from pictures of a person's pets to personal (usually unresearched and unsubstantiated) opinions on gun control and abortion.	Articles from reputable print publications ranging from the *New York Times* to *Sports Illustrated* to the *Economist*.
Appearance	Ranges from obviously personal homepages to pages that look like reliable sources, but are not associated with any reputable organization. Appearance can mislead since organizations such as hate groups can have professional-looking sites.	Little or no advertising because a fee is paid to access resources. Search engines that search *only* the paid database and *not* the general Internet.
Publication schedule	Anytime the person who creates it feels like it.	Databases index and provide full-text access to publications that are in print, so the publication schedule should be the same with some lag time to get it into the computer. Usually updated: Daily, Weekly, Monthly, Quarterly, Biannually Issues are usually identified by volume and/or issue number.
How Useful Academically	Not useful for papers unless the criteria outlined in the web evaluation handout have been met.	Useful for accessing full-text articles online from print publications that are available in the database.
Examples	Search engines like Yahoo, Google, WebCrawler	*EBSCOhost, Proquest, Lexis-Nexis.*

University of St. Thomas

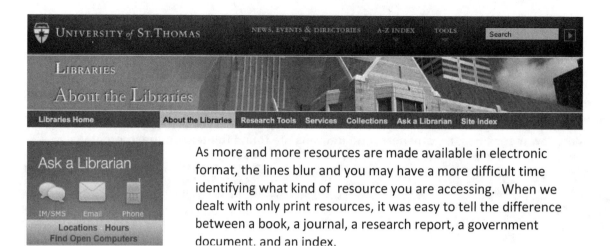

Now, all of these same types of resources are available in an online format and you may not be sure which type you are using. In addition, anyone can create web sites which may or may not include reliable information. However they may still look like the more credible resources available through the web and it can become really confusing.

You may not be sure if you have found actual research information, or just another general web site that someone down the street created because they thought their ideas were interesting.

One way you can identify the value of the information that you have found, is to use the following six criteria for evaluating resources:

- **ACCURACY**
  Are sources of information and factual data listed, and available for cross-checking
- **AUTHORITY**
  Who is responsible for the work and what are their qualifications and associations, and can you verify them?
- **OBJECTIVITY**
  Are biases clearly stated? Are any political/ ideological agenda hidden to disguise its purpose? Do they use a misleading name or other means to do this?
- **CURRENCY**
  How up-to-date is the information?
- **COVERAGE**
  What is the focus of the work?
- **RELEVANCY**
  Does the resource actually cover the topic you are researching?

For more specific information on evaluating different types of resources, see the chart on the "How do you evaluate resources?" web page.

Finding Credible Resources:

In order to find valid information on the web, here are two different types of search tools that you can use:

- **Web Search engines:** these find web sites on particular topics. Remember that anyone can put anything on the web, so you may find a really good government report, an article written by a well-known researcher in a field, a web site created by a group that is biased toward a certain perspective, or a web site created by a 10-year-old in Nebraska.
- **Online databases**: these are resources that we pay to access. They may provide information on what research articles are available on a particular topic, access to some full-text articles in research journals, in magazines, or in newspapers, access to full-text research journals, or statistical tables and reports. Some of these resources are also available in regular print resources (indexes, books, journals), while others may only be available online.

There are advantages to using both of these types of resources. You need to evaluate what kind of information you need and then you can decide what resources to use:

Advantages:

Online Databases	Web Search engines
In-depth content from quality journals	Government information and statistics are readily available
Precision searching using: - Subject headings (descriptors) - Classification codes - Specific searching by title or author	Organizations or special interest groups identify and collect "best" resources
Authority/Editorial process to identify research article--refereed (peer-reviewed)	Provide access to electronic databases
Academic research--published for tenure	New research peer-reviewed journals available only in electronic format
Some articles available in full-text	Mailing lists: groups which discuss specific topics and share information and research
Online library catalog will identify print resources available in local library	News resources or other extremely current information

There are also disadvantages to both types of resources:

Disadvantages:

Online Databases	Web Search engines
Most articles are not available in full-text--journals may not be available in local libraries and may need to be requested through Interlibrary Loan--takes time	Precision searching is not available resulting in thousands, or sometimes millions, of web sites to review
Even if journals are available at the local library, it takes time to locate the resources	Since anyone can put anything on the web, the quality of the resources may be poor and/or at a child's level of research
	Overwhelming amount of information--you must sort the good information out of thousands of web sited identified
	In an effort to protect copyright, most information is NOT made available or accessible on the web
	Biased or incorrect information is mixed with good research sources

Hints to help identify research articles in electronic format:

- Does it list the title of a publication? (journal or book)
- Is there a volume or issue number?
- Does it say something like "originally published in...."?
- Is there a list a resources (a bibliography)? Can the sources listed be verified (do they really exist)?

York College of Pennsylvania

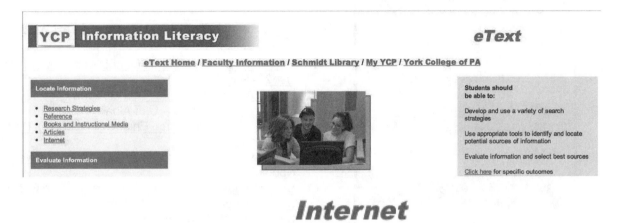

Internet

General Information / Internet Search Tools

Finding Websites using Schmidt Library

Basics :

There are several ways to locate reliable websites using the Schmidt Library. Try using the options below:

1. From the Schmidt Library home page, click on **Finder** in the left-hand navigation menu.Choose Find Websites. From there you can choose to access the following websites and web tools:

   Using Search Tools - provides a list of links to Search Engines, Directories and MetaSearchers.

   Recommended by Librarians - provides a list of general academic websites; also shows directions for searching the Schmidt Library Catalog for websites using keywords or subjects.

   By Subject - lists of recommended websites by subject.
2. Cite Internet Sources

General Information
Overviews

1. Ethics in Computing - NC State U
2. Internet Tutorials -- U of Albany
3. Understanding the World Wide Web -- U of Albany
4. Finding Information on the Internet: A TUTORIAL -- U of California, Berkeley

History of the Internet

1. A Brief History of the Internet -- Internet Society
2. Nerds 2.0.1: A Brief History of the Internet -- PBS

Terms

1. ILC Glossary of Internet Terms
2. Webopedia -- Online Dictionary for terms.

Defining the Nature of the Web 43

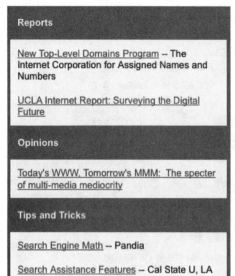

Reports

New Top-Level Domains Program -- The Internet Corporation for Assigned Names and Numbers

UCLA Internet Report: Surveying the Digital Future

Opinions

Today's WWW, Tomorrow's MMM: The specter of multi-media mediocrity

Tips and Tricks

Search Engine Math -- Pandia

Search Assistance Features -- Cal State U, LA

© 2010 York College of Pennsylvania

Focus Questions

What is the Internet?

What is the WWW and how is it distinguished from the Internet?

What kinds of information are likely to be on the **web**? Explain.

What information is NOT available for free on the WWW? Why?

What should you do when you get thousands of hits when you are searching the WWW?

What is the difference between a **web** directory and a search engine?

What are the advantages of human intervention in the creation of **Web** directories?

What is a meta-searcher?

What are advantages of spiders, crawlers, worms, and bots for building search engine databases?

Internet Search Tools

Choosing a Search Tool (Directories, Search Engines)

1. What Kind of Search Engines or Directories Should You Use? -- Pandia
2. Basic Search Techniques -- U of Albany
3. Best Bet Search Tips -- U of Albany
4. How to Choose a Search Engine or Research Database -- U of Albany
5. Choose the Best Search for Your Information Need -- Noodletools
6. Search Engine Showdown Reviews (Search Engines, Subject Directories, News Databases) -- Searchengineshowdown.com

Subject Directories

1. Internet Subject Directories -- U of Albany
2. Internet Subject Directories -- Search Engine Showdown

Search Engines

1. How Search Engines Work --The Spider's Apprentice
2. Internet Search Engines --U of Albany
3. Search Engine FAQs --The Spider's Apprentice
4. How Search Engines Work -- Search Engine Watch
5. Search Engine Features Chart -- Searchengineshowdown.com

Meta-search Engines

1. Metasearch Engines -- U of California, Berkeley
2. Meta Search Engines - U of Albany

Web 2.0

1. 7 Things You Should Know About... - Educause

Invisible/Deep Web

1. Invisible Web -- U of California, Berkeley
2. The Deep Web -- U of Albany

Specialty Search Engines

1. Specialty Search Engines -- Search Engine Watch
2. News Search Engines -- Search Engine Watch

Statistics

1. Search Engine Sizes -- Search Engine Watch
2. Internet Traffic Report

W. Frank Steely Library

Steely Library > Research Help > Tutorials > Basic Tutorials > Research on the Web

Research on the Web

First Step: Choose the Right Tools

Spending hours on the 'Net? Not finding information for your research project? Not sure you can trust the information you're retrieving?

Sometimes you can ease your frustration by using advanced searching techniques. (See Tips and Techniques below for more information.) Frequently, though, it's not a question of mastering search engines. Rather, it's a question of identifying the appropriate tool in the first place. The Internet is wonderful, and can provide material we have never had access to before, but it is not necessarily the first place to go for college-level research. Consider your needs:

Facets of Web Research

Subject Directories vs. Search Engines

Search Engines

Multi-Threaded Search Engines

Organizations and Listservs

Tips and Techniques

Understanding the URL

More Tips

Are you looking for statistics?

The World Wide Web is a terrific source for statistical information (see Steely Library's Research Guide for statistics), but sometimes a statistical handbook is even better. Reference librarians know where to look and are happy to help.

Are you looking for the point of view of a particular group, such as the NRA on gun control?

The Internet is one of the best places to look. Try one of the links to lists of online organizations below.

Do you want the text of a newspaper, magazine or journal article?

The periodicals published on the Web make up a small minority of the periodicals available, and even fewer are available online for free. You can use the new Google Scholar, to identify citations for many periodical articles, but most hits will require a fee to actually see the article. For most magazine and journal articles, you will have better luck with the databases subscribed to by Steely Library, many of which offer full-text articles from both current and past issues.

Do you need brief factual information?

The 'Net is a possibility, although a reference book is often faster and usually more reliable. You can get this kind of information from the third floor Public Service Desk -- call 572-5456 or email us.

Do you need a complete, in-depth study?

BOOKS! Use NKUIRE to find a book on your topic.

Are you looking for information that has been carefully checked for accuracy? Are you seeking reports, critical analysis, or scholarly investigation of a topic?

Your chances of finding complete, reliable information are much better if you use material that is reviewed -- by fact-checkers, editors, or peer reviewers -- before being published. This is true of books, newspaper articles, and magazine articles, and it is especially true of scholarly journal articles. It is most definitely not the case with many WWW sources, as there is very little quality control on the Internet! Your best option is to use a periodical index or library catalog. If you prefer to search the Web, try a Subject Directory rather than a search engine to conduct your search. This will improve your chances of finding reliable web sites. To learn how to judge web sites for yourself, go to Evaluate Web Pages.

Subject Directories vs. Search Engines

Subject directories organize web sites into categories. They are compiled by people, not machines; in this way they differ from search engines. Most subject directories are searchable, but what is actually searched is limited to the contents of the directory. The directories below review sites for quality before linking to them. If you choose to use a less selective directory like Yahoo (which will accept any web page that's submitted), be sure to evaluate your results.

- About: the Human Internet
- Academic Info
- Encyclopedia Britannica Best Web Sites
- INFOMINE
- Internet Scout Project
- Librarian's Index to the Internet
- Price's List of Lists

Search Engines

Search engines electronically seek specific words or phrases, then retrieve documents that match your keywords. They generally retrieve much larger lists of results than subject guides do, because they search a much greater portion of the WWW, and some search every word on a page.

For help choosing a search engine, try Search Engine Watch. Search engines aim at quantity rather than quality. For this reason you should carefully evaluate any web sites you find.

- Alltheweb
- AltaVista
- Excite
- Google
- HotBot
- Lycos

Multi-Threaded Search Engines

Also known as meta-search engines, they search multiple databases simultaneously, using a single interface. For a comparison and explanation, see Meta-Search Engines from the U.C. Berkeley Teaching Library. The disadvantage to using multi-threaded search engines is that they lack advanced searching features.

- Ask Jeeves
- DogPile
- Ixquick
- Metacrawler

Organizations and Listservs

Organizations can be fruitful sources for position statements, journals and newsletters, and links to high quality resources on the Internet. Listservs and discussion groups allow you to enter an online discussion on a specific topic.

Scholarly Societies Project

A directory of web sites maintained by or for scholarly societies across the world.

Associations on the Net

A directory of professional and trade associations, cultural and art organizations, political parties and advocacy groups, labor unions, academic societies, think tanks and research institutions.

American Council of Learned Societies

A federation of 61 national scholarly organizations in the humanities and related social sciences.

Google Group

Search for Usenet newsgroups from this site.

Tips and Techniques for Using Search Engines
Key Word Searching:

Search engines, unlike library catalogs, periodical indexes, and Internet subject guides, do not search by consistent subject headings. They rely instead on key words. Search engines can only find words that are actually entered in your query. For example, a search for medieval would not return any documents that used "middle ages" instead.

Search engines also do not distinguish between words that are spelled the same way, but mean something different (physical plants, manufacturing plants, garden plants). This often results in hits that are completely irrelevant to your query.

Boolean Searching and Proximity Searching:

In order to search effectively, you need to understand how to refine your search by combining search terms. The basic Boolean operators AND, OR and NOT are used to combine terms in most search engines.

Each search engine is different. Be sure to read the HELP screens for each search engine you employ. Search Engine Watch offers a chart comparing search features. See HotBot's Advanced Search Features for an example of a search engine's help screen.

See our guide to Boolean Searching for more instruction

Understanding the URL

The URL, or address, of a web page is the most direct way to search for information on the WWW. The URL takes you directly to the page you want to see. Here is an example of a URL:

http://library.nku.edu/howfindbook.html

Here is how they are constructed: transfer protocol :// servername . domain / directory / subdirectory / filename . filetype

Domain types are as follows:

- .edu: an educational institution
- .org: a nonprofit organization
- .com: a commercial enterprise
- .net: an Internet Service Provider (ISP)
- .gov: a governmental body
- .mil: a military body

There are also domains for individual countries; for example, .ca is Canada and .uk is the United Kingdom.

More Tips

Search Engine Watch

> Click on "Web Searching Tips" for excellent searching help, reviews and news about search engines, and a comparison chart.

The Spider's Apprentice: A Helpful Guide To Web Search Engines

> Offers searching tips, information about how search engines work, and comparisons of popular search engines.

Recommended Search Strategy: Search With Peripheral Vision

Search Engines: What they Are, How They Work, and Practical Suggestions for Getting the Most Out of Them

Windweaver's Search Guide

Tarleton State University Libraries   Unit 3

INTERNET MATERIALS: PURPOSE & USES

Internet Materials take a wide variety of forms and require various methods of access.

As used in this discussion, the term Internet materials applies to items that can be accessed using online search engines or directories, following web page links, or typing specific URLs. In general, these online materials are also free.

One of the main features of the Internet is the ability to quickly link an item to other related information. Also, the Internet offers information beyond plain text, including sounds, images, and video. Usually, information on the Internet is accessed using a browser.

Anyone with an Internet account can post information on the Internet; therefore it offers a wealth of information. However, the ease with which information can be made publicly available also means that special care must be taken when evaluating information that is freely available on the Internet. More information about evaluating Internet materials is provided in Unit 8.

The following list shows some reasons to use Internet materials as research sources:
- **to find current news and information,**
- **to locate information about companies, industries, and trends,**
- **to quickly access facts, numbers, and definitions,**
- **to locate both expert and popular opinions, and**
- **to find information from all levels of government.**

◀ **Newspapers: Purpose & Uses**   **Using Primary/Secondary Sources** ▶
Library Orientation Site Index
Updated 7/2004

University Libraries
Division of Academic Affairs
© 2010 Tarleton State University

College of Mount St. Joseph

INSIDE THE MOUNT   Quick Links   ▼   🔍 Search Site   GO

Academics | Departments | Campus Life | Technology & Tools

Using Web Search Tools

The **World Wide Web (WWW)** is a collection of hyper-linked multimedia documents stored on computers worldwide. By using a software application called a Web browser, you can view Web documents, also known as Web pages.

Search tools are computer programs that search for information on the World Wide Web. They allow you to search the Web by keyword or by browsing subject lists. **Subject directories** assign sites to specific topic categories based on the site's content and are good for searching general topics. Keyword or **general search engines** produce an index of all the text on the sites they examine; they are better for very specific information. **Meta-search engines** allow you to search a number of databases and engines simultaneously.

Most search tools are programmed to retrieve all documents containing any of your search terms. Results are ranked by placing documents that contain more of your search terms higher on the results list. Be aware that some search tools use "paid placement", where sites pay a fee to be positioned near the top of the results list.

Placing quotation marks around search terms retrieves a phrase or series of words in the exact order you type them -- **"great barrier reef"**. A plus sign in front of a search term means that the term must be present in the document to retrieve it -- **billiard +rules**. A minus sign in front of a search term means that the term will not be in the documents retrieved -- **magazine -computer**.

For more help with using Web search tools, connect to Web Search Tips.

From the **Archbishop Alter Library** home page, **Search the Web** takes you to Search Engines & Directories, Metacrawlers & Metasearch Engines, Specialty Subject Search Engines, Web Sites listed by Subject, Web Search Tips , & Evaluating Web Sites. From there you can connect to search tool and learn more about them.

Archbishop Alter Library
College of Mount St. Joseph
5701 Delhi Road – Cincinnati, Ohio 45233-1671

*Since the Internet is now a common medium for information these days,
let's be sure some concepts about the Internet are clear.*

The Internet delivers information in many different ways: email, the World Wide Web, FTP, Telnet and others.

The Internet is now an *international network* that connects people, organizations, and companies through their computers.

The Internet began in the 1950's at the Advanced Research Projects Agency -- a department of the US government.

One of its original purposes was to allow professors and researchers at widely separated institutions to share information quickly and easily.

*and no, the Internet is not a government conspiracy.
In fact, the Internet has no government at all!*

Your computer uses special software called browsers,
(such as Internet Explorer or Firefox) to connect to the Internet.
Browsers allow you to use your computer to retrieve information stored on other
computers, and puts that information in a form that you can view or read.

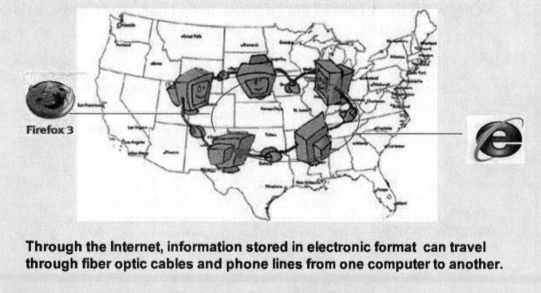

Firefox 3

Through the Internet, information stored in electronic format can travel
through fiber optic cables and phone lines from one computer to another.

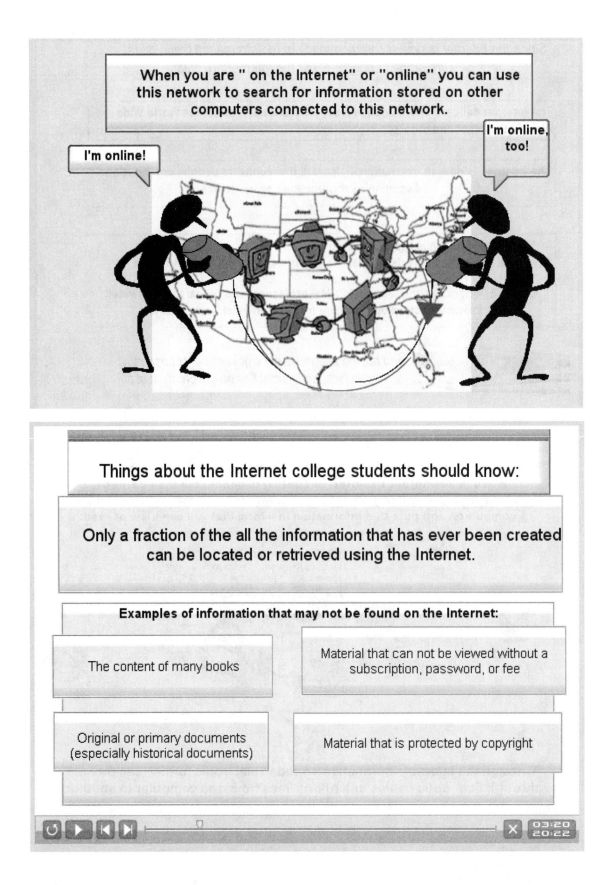

Things about the Internet college students should know:

Don't assume everyone means the same thing when they use the term "the Internet."

When a professor uses that expression, be sure you know exactly what is meant or ask for clarification.

The Internet *can* link you to more sites with information than you can humanly view, but you are responsbile for deciding if the information on those sites is accurate, up-to-date, and authoritative.

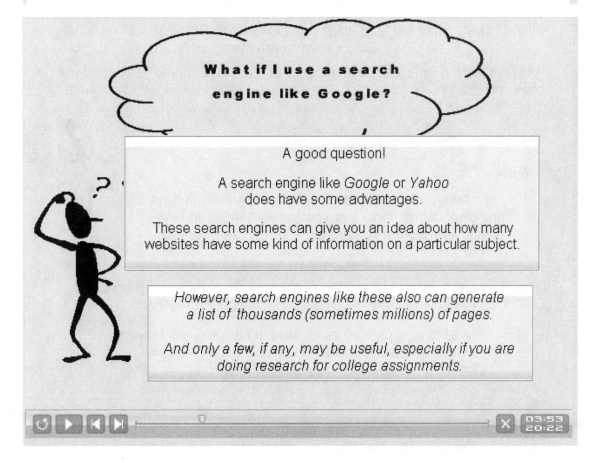

What if I use a search engine like Google?

A good question!

A search engine like *Google* or *Yahoo* does have some advantages.

These search engines can give you an idea about how many websites have some kind of information on a particular subject.

However, search engines like these also can generate a list of thousands (sometimes millions) of pages.

And only a few, if any, may be useful, especially if you are doing research for college assignments.

03:53
20:22

Click the arrow beside the unfinished statement and select the correct ending.

The Internet___

⊙ A) enables world-wide communication.

○ B) is exactly the same as the World Wide Web.

○ C) is an agency of the United States government.

Submit

Clear

That is correct! The international network that is the Internet allows information to be transmitted in many different formats.
However, no "Internet police" or universal laws contol the Internet.

Click anywhere to continue.

Question 1 of 6

When most people say "the Internet" they are talking about places on it that can be seen by anyone.

Many of the scholarly journals and books you are expected to use for college research assignments are simply not available in such places on the Internet.

You **can** use the Internet to finds lots of information.

But---

---- among all the millions of web pages, ads, chat rooms and other distractions, it is sometimes hard to find the **quality information** *you are expected to use in college.*

For that reason, many of your professors may discourage you from using publically available websites on the Internet for research.

Almost all of your professors will want to be sure you know how to use the information sources discussed in this tutorial before (or in addition to) looking for information on websites.

19:31
20:22

Louisiana State University at Alexandria | 8100 Hwy 71 South | Alexandria, LA 71302

Search Engines and Directories

http://www.gocee.com

/eureka/

Eureka! gives lists to search engines with an explanation of each search engine and a link to it.

http://www.excite.com

Web Portal with Search Engine

http://www.google.com

Go to **Advanced Search,** then click on **Advanced Search Tips** to see hints such as:

- Enclose world in double-quotes to force the words to appear together in all returned documents

- Prefix your query word or phrase with a" -" to make Google ignore all pages containing it.

Winthrop University ©
701 Oakland Avenue
Rock Hill, SC 29733, USA

Internet Searching Tools

The following tools and services are designed for searching the Internet for sites and resources.
Note: These tools are ranked based on their interface, versatility, and ease of use. The How to Search the Internet provides useful tools to learn about Internet searching. The Best of the Rest provides an eclectic list of other useful resources for a variety of Internet searching needs.

Quick Links to the Top Twelve Search Tools by Category
Click the header for a short description of each tool and a link to the Help menu.

SEARCH TOOLS	METASEARCH TOOLS	SUBJECT DIRECTORIES
Google Advanced Search	Ixquick Metasearch	INFOMINE
Yahoo! Advanced Search	Dogpile	Academic Info
Ask Advanced Search	Search.com	Best Information on the Net
All the Web Advanced Search	Surfwax	Internet Public Library
Bing Advanced Search	Clusty	The Scout Report Archives
Exalead Advanced Search	Mamma	Digital Librarian
Alta Vista Advanced Search	Kartoo	About.com
Gigablast Advanced Search	Beaucoup	Open Directory Project
Lycos Advanced Search	Highway 61	World Wide Web Virtual Library
HotBot Advanced Search	Metacca	Complete Planet:The Deep Web
Quintura	Turbo10	A1WebDirectory.org
Snap	Findelio	JoeAnt

Southern Oregon University

HOW TO SEARCH THE INTERNET

Finding Information on the Internet: A Tutorial

BARE BONES 101: A Web Search Tutorial

Web Search Tutorial by Pandia

Web Search from About.comBest Search Tools Chart

Graduated Search Strategy

How to Choose a Search Engine

Tips for Effective Internet Searching

Evaluating Web Resources

Internet Research: Searching the World Wide Web

Search Engine Showdown

Search Engine Watch

THE BEST OF THE REST

Google Books

Google Scholar

Research-It

http://www.findarticles.comGoogle

UncleSam

Wikipediahttp://babel.altavista.com/

LibrarySpot

HotSheet

Refdesk.com

FindArticles

Essential Links (EL)

How Stuff Works

Search Engine Colossus

© 2008 Lenn and Dixie Hannon Library
1250 Siskiyou Blvd., Ashland, Oregon 97520

INTERNET SEARCH TOOLS

Internet Search Tools, as used here, refers to online tools used to locate and create listings of Internet sites. These tools help researchers find information that is not in subscription databases, behind firewalls, or in other unattainable areas of the Internet. At times, the information will be free. However, in many instances, the information is only available for a fee.

Internet search tools come in five primary forms: search engines, meta search tools, directories, pathfinders/research guides, and searchable databases.

Search Engines use computer programs called "spiders" or "robots" to compile Internet pages and then scan these pages when users enter search terms in the search engine. Each search engine only scans the pages it has compiled, not the entire Internet. Therefore, it is always a good idea to use more than one search engine when looking for information on the Internet.

Most search engines offer "advanced search" or "guided search" interfaces that let users search by phrase, combine searches, limit searches, etc. Therefore, they help searchers locate more relevant information.

However, given the number of pages on the Internet (over a billion and growing), search results lists are often quite long, which decreases research efficiency. Also, search engines do not necessarily list search results starting with the best ones. Many different guidelines come into play when search results are listed--including paid placement and paid inclusion. Examples of search engines are **AltaVista** and **AlltheWeb**. Other search engines like **Excite**, **Google**, and **Yahoo** offer the combined features of search engines and directories (see below).

⬆ **TOP**

Meta Search Tools simultaneously search the sites compiled by several search engines, which can save you time when conducting searches that require broad coverage. However, meta search tools usually offer limited control over search options and may not search as thoroughly as using individual search engines would. Examples of meta search tools are **MetaCrawler**, **Dogpile**, **KillerInfo**, and **Ixquick**.

 **Directories** offer lists of Internet sites organized by subject and are created by people who review sites to determine their worth before listing them (or not). Directories list fewer sites about a subject than search engines because directories are selective and the sites have been reviewed. However, this selectivity increases the probability that a listed site will be relevant and useful.

Directories are fairly easy to navigate. Users browse the categories and follow links to find desired material. However, this process can be time-consuming, and users must clearly understand where a site might be listed in order to find it. Many directories also offer search mechanisms to help users locate listed sites. Example directories include **Argus Clearinghouse**, **Internet Public Library**, **dmoz** (the Open Directory project), and **The WWW Virtual Library**.

⬆ **TOP**

 **Pathfinders & Research Guides** are similar to directories, but are subject specific. They are usually compiled by experts in a field or subject-specialist librarians who search the Internet, evaluate web sites, and compile lists for a specific field, subject, discipline, etc. Many libraries, companies, and professional organizations offer online pathfinders and research guides.

Example research guides are the Tarleton libraries' **Human Resource Management** and **Business & Accounting** guides which offer links to Tarleton library resources (catalog and databases) and to lists of relevant Internet sites.

 **Free Searchable Databases** can be good sources of information, but are often not found by search engines or listed in subject directories. You can sometimes find them while browsing the Internet. More likely, you'll find them listed in directories of searchable databases, such as **The Invisible Web Directory** and U.S. Department of Education's **Cross-Site Indexing Project**.

⬆ TOP

Internet search tools are useful

- when you are brainstorming ideas for a research topic,

- when you need current information about companies, industries, people, countries, etc.

- when you want to locate information regarding all levels of government,

- when you need international information that is unavailable locally, and

- when you want to locate online periodicals to retrieve articles (if they are available either free or for a fee).

Finally, researchers should remember that some search engines offer "paid placement" (determines how far up a results list a site is listed) and that no expertise is needed to post an Internet page. Therefore special care must be taken when evaluating information freely available on the Internet. Unit 8 offers more in-depth information about evaluating Internet sites.

⬅ **Library Databases**   **Matching Search Tools & Info Needs** ➡

Dakota State University

Internet Search: Subject Directories, Search Engines, & More

Contents: [Subject Directories] .... [Search Engines: General   Niche   Question-answering   Blog] .... [Meta Search Tools]
[Find Today's News] .... [Find People & Businesses] .... [Find Reviews of Web sites]
[Evaluating Internet Sources] .... [Finding Good Sites For Kids]

Introduction -- You can find information on the Internet by using one or more of the many available subject directories and search engines listed below. But watch out! All subject directories and search engines are not equal. Which one works best will vary depending on the nature of the particular information you need. One that works well on one search may work very poorly on another. To improve your search results, learn more about subject directories and search engines.

Anyone can "publish" on the Web, no matter how qualified, how ignorant, or how biased they might be. Therefore, the the information found varies from bogus to scholarly. Be wary of what you find and improve the quality of the sources you use by learning more about evaluating materials on the Internet.

Subject Directories -- provide a good place to start when searching for information about broad topics or when browsing the Internet because the sites included are selected by people rather than by search engine "robots."

- To learn more, read about subject directories.

Links to some of the better subject directories:

General subject directories -- less selective	
About.com	http://www.about.com/
CompletePlanet	http://aip.completeplanet.com -- Directory of the deep web. "A comprehensive listing of dynamic searchable databases. Find databases with highly relevant documents that cannot be crawled or indexed by surface web search engines."
Open Directory Project	http://www.dmoz.org --The **Open Directory Project** is the largest, most comprehensive human-edited directory of the Web. It is constructed and maintained by a vast, global community of volunteer editors.

Yahoo directory or Yahoo home	http://dir.yahoo.com/ -- The Yahoo directory has been the best-known & largest human-compiled directory of the Web. However, the search on the Yahoo home page (www.yahoo.com) no longer searches the Yahoo directory but instead is a Google search of the Web. To get to the human-compiled categories, go to the Yahoo Directory link.
Google directory	http://www.google.com/dirhp -- Google's directory is based on the Open Directory project

General subject directories -- more selective

 BUBL http://www.bubl.ac.uk/link/ -- Internet resources covering all academic subject areas are selected, evaluated, catalogued and described. Links are checked and fixed each month.

 **Internet Public Library** http://www.ipl.org/ -- search or browse Internet resources covering all subject areas. Primarily selected by librarians and library science graduate students.

 **Librarians' Internet Index** http://lii.org/ -- human-compiled; Internet resources selected and evaluated by librarians for their usefulness to users of public libraries

 **Scout Report** http://scout.cs.wisc.edu/archives/ -- search or browse the "archives" of selected and reviewed web sites chosen by the editorial board of Scout Report

Academic/scholarly subject directories

 **Infomine** http://infomine.ucr.edu/ -- scholarly web sites

 **Intute** http://www.intute.ac.uk/ -- Intute (Formerly RDN:Resource Discovery Network) is the UK's free national gateway to Internet resources for the learning, teaching and research community. The service links to resources via a series of subject-based information gateways (or hubs). Intute gathers resources which are carefully selected by subject specialists in partner institutions.

Search engines -- allow you to search for keywords in order to find information on narrow topics and to find the web pages of specific organizations, agencies, or people.

- To learn more about using search engines effectively, read about search engines.
- To learn more about the search engines listed above, read Greg Notess' **Search Engine Showdown**. Note the Features Chart, a summary table showing which search techniques can be used in the major search engines
- For search engine news, use **Pandia Search Engine Detective** to search the top search engine blogs, discussion lists, news sites, etc.

Links to some of the better Search Engines:

General Search Engines

Google   http://www.google.com/ --Crawler-based & comprehensive (large) database. **Ranking of results by popularity** helps find good sites when searching broad topics. Offers a variety of advanced and other search options; for example, image search or U.S. government search

Clusty   http://clusty.com -- Vivisimo's search site called Clusty sorts results into folders to **group similar items (clusters)**. For those that like the clustering, meta-search approach, Clusty is well worth a visit.

Yahoo! Search   http://search.yahoo.com/ -- Crawler-based, comprehensive (large) database with a variety of search options. (Yahoo purchased Alta Vista and All the Web in 2003 and in March 2004 these search engines were re-designed to return results similar to Yahoo Search). Uses its own database.

Live Search   http://www.live.com/ -- It is the successor to MSN Search. Sometimes called Windows Live Search. Launched in September 2006, it uses its own, unique database. Use the table of contents on the left to navigate this review.

Gigablast   http://www.gigablast.com/ -- Gigablast is the only search engine indexing meta tags beyond just the meta description and meta keywords that some others index. After a search limit by the provided tags.

Ask.com http://www.ask.com -- The search engine formerly known as Ask Jeeves has changed greatly from its early days as a question answer matching service to being a real Web search engine using a database originally developed by Teoma.

exalead one:websearch   http://www.exalead.com/search - Exalead is a newer search engine from France. It offers a unique and different approach to presenting results. A database of crawled Web pages and an image database.

Lycos   **http://www.lycos.com** -- based on the Open Directory project (which uses volunteer editors to collect sites into categories)

Niche search engines.   These search engines focus on a specific subject or type of information. Reducing the search universe makes the list of search results more manageable and on target. Here are just a few examples.

Asiaco   http://www.asiabot.com/ -- search the Internet for topics related to **Asia.**

CiteSeer http://citeseer.ist.psu.edu/ -- Search not only indexed **scientific** documents but also the citations they contain.

Google Scholar http://scholar.google.com -- "Google Scholar enables you to search specifically for **scholarly** literature, including peer-reviewed papers, theses, books, preprints, abstracts and technical reports from all broad areas of research."

OAIster http://oaister.umdl.umich.edu/o/oaister/ -- collection of freely available, difficult-to-access, academically-oriented digital resources.

Topix http://www.topix.net -- **news** search engine. For local news, enter zip code or city/state in search box at top.

Windows Live Academic http://academic.live.com/ -- similar to Google Scholar. [Only physics, electrical engineering and computer science - April 2006]

Question Answering engines. These search engines are designed to answer questions presented in natural language

BrainBoost http://www.brainboost.com/ -- Finds answers to your questions posed in plain English (e.g., Where is Iraq? How many calories are in a cheeseburger?)

Blog search engines. These search engines are designed to search and find information in blogs. For more, see Big List of Blog Search Engines

Meta search tools -- allow you to search more than one search engine at a time.

- While metasearch may save you from selecting a specific search engine, **metasearching also has important disadvantages**.
- To learn more about metacrawlers, read UC Berkeley Library's Meta-Search Engines. They "recommend directly searching each search engine and **recommend AGAINST using meta-searchers."**

Links to some of the meta search tools:

Clusty http://clusty.com -- sorts results into folders to **group similar items (clusters)**. Searches do not include Google or Yahoo.

Dogpile http://www.dogpile.com/ -- Google, Yahoo, MSN LiveSearch, and Ask

Kartoo http://www.kartoo.com/   visual metasearch engine

UJIKO http://www.ujiko.com/ "... **UJIKO** evolves with your expertise

SurfWax http://www.surfwax.com/

New tools for fighting information overload using visual methods for displaying & categorizing results

Grokker   http://www.groxis.com

Plumb Design Visual http://www.visualthesaurus.com
Thesaurus
Kartoo http://www.kartoo.com/   visual metasearch engine

UJIKO http://www.ujiko.com/ "... **UJIKO** evolves with your expertise: **The more you use it, the more functions it is able to offer** ....Starting from the second level, UJIKO displays in the center of the screen **sets of themes**: just click on one of these to improve / refine your search. Some of these topics are coloured and are linked to small bricks with the same color: these indicate which sites are associated with a specific theme. UJIKO is another product from the developers of Kartoo.

Tools for finding today's news

Google News   http://news.google.com/

Pandia Newsfinder   http://www.pandia.com/news/ -- metasearch engine will get headlines, summaries and links to articles from news sites on the Internet, including BBC, CNN, MSNBC, Yahoo, The Wall Street Journal, The Washington Post, NewsHub and Moreover

Tools for finding people and businesses -- allow you to do find one or more of the following about people or businesses: e-mail addresses, phone numbers, mailing addresses, and additional information.

Link to one of these:	*Source*	*Information provided*
WhoWhere? People Finder	http://www.whowhere.lycos.com/	-- search person's name to find address and phone, e-mail, web pages

(Lycos)

People Search http://people.yahoo.com/ -- search name to find phone, address,
(Yahoo) & e-mail

Switchboard http://www.switchboard.com/

ATT Anywho Info http://www.anywho.com/ -- In "Find a Name," search person's
name to find mail address, phone number, map. Or use "Find a
Business, to find a business."

Reverse Lookup http://www.anywho.com/rl.html --search phone number to find
(ATT Anywho) name, mail address, map

Find reviews of web sites. Newsletters and journals that review web sites are listed
below. See also the section above on "Subject Directories that rate and review sites." Newsletters
usually have a search option and/or an archive of back issues to locate the reviews.

Newsletters: Netsurfer Digest

Scout Report

Journals: College & Research Libraries News

Evaluating Internet sources -- is necessary when using the Web for research, because
no one is controlling the quality of the material placed there. Although a list of search results can
be retrieved quickly with a search engine, sorting the good from the bad, the current from the out-
of-date, the bogus from the reliable, the scholarly from the popular, and the biased from the
objective can take considerable time. To learn to evaluate Internet sources:

- First, read Evaluating Materials on the Internet.
- For additional help, read "Evaluation Criteria" (by Susan Beck, New Mexico State
  University), Evaluating Internet Research Sources (by Robert Harris, Southern California
  College), and Evaluating Web Resources (by Jan Alexander & Marsha Ann Tate, Widener
  University).
- Then visit Consumer WebWatch -- to learn about their five guidelines for websites that
  want to establish credibility with consumers:
  http://www.consumerwebwatch.org/bestpractices/index.html

Karl E. Mundt Library & Learning Commons | Dakota State University | Madison, SD 57042

TischLibrary

Search Resources ▾   Get Help   ▾   Use Our Services ▾   Tisch and You ▾   About Tisch   ▾

Wednesday, March 3rd, 2010

Recommended Search Engines
Home > Get Help > Finding & Searching > Recommended Search Engines

SHARE

Search This Site

[   ] Search

Academic Directories and Search Engines

If you need to find scholarly material on the web, try using search engines or web directories that specialize in academic or educational websites.

Librarian's Index
to the Internet
http://lii.org
Search Tips

The Librarian's Index to the Internet links to digital collections and online exhibits on a variety of academic topics.

You can explore the sites listed by browsing subject categories or by searching for websites relevant to your topic. Lii.org frequently creates theme-based collections about recent events such as "War and Peace Resources Related to the Current Iraq Crisis".

Ask.com
http://www.ask.com

Ask.com incorporates a variety of search tools including image searching, maps and directions, and news search. The advanced search page (make "advanced search page" link to http://www.ask.com/webadvanced) allows you to limit your search by the date a web page was last updated, geographical region, domain name, and more.

Infomine
http://infomine.ucr.edu

Built by librarians, Infomine is "a virtual library of Internet resources relevant to faculty, students, and research staff at the university level."
You can search Infomine for scholarly web resources in Biological, Agricultural & Medical Sciences, Social Sciences & Humanities, Business and Economics, Visual & Performing Arts, and more.

Internet Public Library
http://www.ipl.org

The Internet Public Library has an online reference center with links to dictionaries, encyclopedias, and other reference materials. The subject collections cover Arts & Humanities, Law, Government, and Political Science, Science & Technology, and more.

Scout Report Archives
http://scout.wisc.edu/archives
Search Tips

The Internet Scout selects and annotates websites of interest to the higher education community. The scout archives are searchable by keyword, and can also be browsed by Library of Congress subject headings. From the Univ. of Wisconsin-Madison.

Voice of the Shuttle
http://vos.ucsb.edu
Search Tips

From the University of California, Santa Barbara, Voice of the Shuttle is a directory that provides access to scholarly websites for research in the humanities.
You can browse through links by subject area (Art & Art History, Gender Studies, Literature, Media Studies, etc.) or you can search Voice of the Shuttle for a topic such as Zora Neale Hurston.

Scirus
www.scirus.com
Search Tips

If you need to find websites for a research topic in the sciences, use Scirus.com. Scirus searches the web for scientific information, and searches some science journals in addition to science oriented websites. The advanced search in Scirus.com allows you to limit your search to specific types of science information (conference proceedings, patents, scientists' homepages, etc.) or by subject area (life sciences, social and behavioral sciences, etc.)

Scirus will rewrite your search, if using different syntax will likely provide you with better results. Most searches in Scirus will also display related keywords that you could use to refine your search.
Example: A search in Scirus for string theory will give you a list of results from the web and science journals (many of which require the subscription access that Tisch Library provides for selected journals), along with other keywords like "black holes", "cosmology", and "superstring theory."

Search Multiple Search Engines

Dogpile
http://dogpile.com/

Dogpile searches Yahoo, Google, MSN, and Ask Jeeves. You can also use Dogpile to find audio, video, news items, and yellow page listings. The advanced search allows you to limit by domain name, language, and date.

General Search Engines

Google www.google.com Search Tips	Google has many advanced search options that will help you find useful information. • Advanced searching in Google - The advanced search in Google allows you to limit your search by domain name, for example specifying that you only want .edu pages. • Google U.S. Government - A Google search of U.S. government websites only. This search engine is useful if you are researching current issues or controversial topics. Many government agencies maintain informative webpages with detailed documents and reports freely available online.
GoogleScholar Google Scholar	Google Scholar is a new beta search engine from Google that is designed to help people find scholarly material on the web. Although it is too early to tell for sure what portion of scholarly material may be included in Google Scholar, it may be useful for locating material such as research studies funded by the government, scholarly prepublication article archives, and "grey literature," -- material that may be scholarly but not published through traditional publishing channels. Some of the material you find on Google Scholar may not be available for free via Google Scholar, but may be available to you as a member of the Tufts University community. In order to take advantage of being a "Tufts person," search Google Scholar using the link on the Databases and Articles list, or just use this link: http://www.library.tufts.edu/ezproxy/ezproxy.asp?LOCATION=GoogleScholar. If when you are using Google Scholar you find a citation for an article and an option to buy it, double check the Tufts Catalog and the Electronic Journals List to see if we subscribe. If not, use our ILLiad document delivery service to request copies of articles.
Yahoo search.yahoo.com	Yahoo allows you to search for webpages, images, news, and local information. The advanced search page allows you to limit by language, domain name, file format, and country of origin.

University
·OF·
COLORADO
AT COLORADO SPRINGS
UCCS

ASK US
719-255-3296 | refdesk@uccs.edu

Kraemer Family Library

Search UCCS for   Go

Find Resources   Get Help   Library Services   Library Info

Web Search Engines

A list of suggest web search engines and information on setting preferences in search engines like Google Scholar, Scirus and more.

Scholarly Web Search Engines

- Google Scholar
- Scirus
- AgEcon Search
  Research in agriculture
  and applied economics.

- INFOMINE
- WWW Virtual Library
- RefSeek (Beta)

General Search Engines

- Alta Vista
- Dogpile
- Excite
- Google
- Hakia (Beta)

- Lycos Search
- Metacrawler
- Yahoo!
- iTools
- Search.com

Setting Search Preferences

Some web search engines allow UCCS students, staff and faculty to connect to Library resources directly from their web searches. For example, if you are searching in Google Scholar and find a journal article you want to read, but can't get full-text of, by setting search preferences, you can automatically connect to the Library's electronic and print holdings to see if you can get the full-text from the Library.

1. On the opening screen of Google Scholar select the link for Scholar Preferences.
2. Click the box that says "open search results in a new browser window".
3. In the search box type: University of Colorado at Colorado Springs.
4. Click on Find Library.
5. Click on Save preferences.

Note: If you are off campus using Google Scholar, you need to connect to the Library VPN for this to work.

Ready Reference: Search Engines

Search Engines -- Search the Web by Word or Phrase

Search engines create their listings using automated software without evaluating the contents. Use a search engine to find information on very specific topics that require searching with unique terms, for examples: "aromatherapy" or "Joe DiMaggio." Domain names (such as .edu, .gov, .org, .au, .de) can be used to limit searches in most search engines.

Google

Popular and dominant by a huge margin (1 Trillion indexed Web pages currently), Google sprouts new features and "experiments" almost daily.

Google (Advanced Search)

You can combine or exclude search terms or phrases and limit by language, date, domain, or format.

Yahoo!

With the largest index after Google, Yahoo should be checked too because competing search engine indexes do not completely overlap.

Bing (Microsoft)

Bing may owe its rank as the 3rd most used search engine to the world dominance of its owner's software. (Google's index is still far larger.)

alltheweb

allthe web is actually Yahoo, but you may prefer its spartan interface - quite a contrast to Yahoo's own. Also provides a useful method of limiting by date.

Ask.com

Results are ranked by subject popularity, which is not ideal for serious research. Original for its "natural language" search option (now common), Ask.com struggles for distinction.

MetaSearch Engines – Search Several Engines at Once

Everything on the Web can *not* yet be found by Google. In fact, all the search engine indexes combined, cover only about 6% of all the Web pages out there. Moreover, these indexes do not completely overlap, so you may find more by searching several. "Meta-Search" engines (more accurately, "multi-engines," like those listed below, let to use several search engines at once. Although complex searching is not available with these engines, they provide a good starting place.

Clusty

Clusty "clusters" results by subject subdivisions. Good for topical and current event searching.

Dogpile

(InfoSpace) Aggregates results from the 4 largest search engines. Identifies source of each hit but does not reveal the total number of hits. Dogpile may have the worst name, but may also be the least gimmicky.

Ixquick

Brings "top 10" from each search engine, aggregates results, and eliminates duplicates. Its video search engine is very fast. A major claim: Ixquick protects your privacy by deleting the "tracks" you leave behind when searching. Most search engines (Ixquick claims) gather and sometimes sell this information and / or don't secure it from identity thieves.

Subject-Specific Focused Search Engines

Google Scholar

Beta test version. Finds scholarly sources including articles. If the full text is not available, the article may be available to Oneonta students and faculty either in print, in library databases (such as **Academic Search Premier**) or through Interlibrary Loan.

Google Uncle Sam

Searches U.S. Government sites. (Nno ads!)

Science.gov

A selection of science sites from federal agencies.

Scirus

Searches over 200 million science-related web pages, as well as peer-reviewed journals

Citeseer

Full-text scholarly scientific articles. You can trace the works the author has cited AND what works have cited that article. Serious Science.

Google Books (Advanced Search)

Includes full text for many out-of-copyright books (generally 1923 or earlier).

Google Custom Search (CSE)

Google allows you to "design" your own search engine, automating the search of websites you regularly use.

Internet Directories – Browse the Web by Subject

Humans select, sometimes evaluate, and organize (by subject) the listings in a directory. Use a directory to browse and to find the "best" sites on a general or popular topic.

Open Directory Project
Large, briefly annotated directory. Google Directory is based on the *Open Directory Project*.

Librarians' Index to the Internet

Small, but carefully selected, high quality sites with excellent annotations.

Yahoo!

Large, not well annotated, and a little hard to find. One of the first, it's useful for popular and commercial topics, but entries, sadly, can be dated or enemic.

Academic Directories

Academic Info
Selective, annotated "college and research level Internet resources."

Infomine

"Scholarly Internet Resource Collections" is the subtitle. Often refered to, "quirky" may be the best description of this directory maintained by the University of California, Riverside. It may or may not work for you (figuratively or literally).

Intute

It claims to be a "...free online service providing you with a database of hand selected Web resources for education and research." You can limit your search to Arts & Humanities, Health & Life Sciences, Science, Engineering & Technology, the Social Sciences, or any combination. Based in the UK.

VoS - Voice of the Shuttle

"A structured and briefly annotated guide to online resources" focusing on the humanities.

Sources of Informal Information (that may lead to "hard info")

Omgil

Searches through discussion lists dedicated to almost any topic that's being "discussed" on the Web

Boardtracker

Tracks discussions in online "bulletin boards."

Boardreader

The same, but will also search video, images, and Twitter

Google Blogsearch

Google again, to answer: is someone blogging on the topic of your research?

Search.wikia.com

Because wikis are now where a lot of data gathers.

Tutorials on How to Search the Web

Recommended Search Strategy
Step-by-step searching strategy from UC Berkeley Library.

Searchenginez: Web Search Tutorial

Handy tips for web searching, along with links to popular subject search engines.

The Search Engine Business

If you want to know about search engines and the search engine industry, few objective, non-commercial web sites are also current.

Search Engine Showdown

Maintained for years by Greg Notess, it fails to keep current. But he is writing search engine news for *Online Magazine*. Find abstracts to his past columns at **http://www.infotoday.com/online/** OR the whole text by searching in **Academic Search Premier**, using "Notess" in the author field (It's a drop-down menu) and "Online" in the Journal Name field.

James M. Milne Library • SUNY College at Oneonta • Oneonta, New York 13820

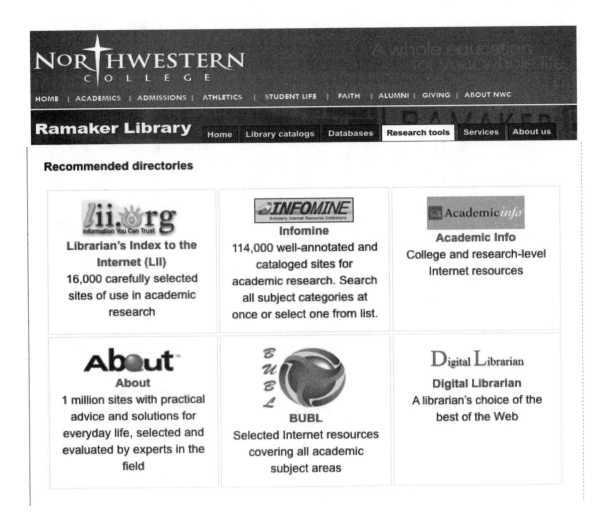

Search Strategies

GRINNELL COLLEGE LIBRARIES

| More Resources | Get Help | Collections | About Us | Ask a Librarian (OFFLINE) |

Search the Library Catalog | Grinnell College > Libraries > Research > Instruction Guides > Search Engines Tips | Printer-Friendly

Search Engine Tips

Internet Search Strategies

Internet search engines provide us with a way to search for and access information on the Internet. Given the broad range of search engines currently available, it is important to understand what portion of the Internet each search engine covers, and how to use each search engine in the most efficient way.

At present, the search engine Google appears to be the most commonly used basic search engine. AltaVista, HotBot/Lycos, AskJeeves, and Yahoo are some of the other frequently-used search engines. Unfortunately, these different search engines were not programmed to respond to queries in exactly the same way, which means that the searcher must understand a slightly different set of "search rules" when using each search engine. Some of the variations in search rules have been outlined below.

Carefully Select Key Words/Concepts

Regardless of which search engine you choose, the success of your search will be determined by your choice of search terms. Before you begin, consider your question or topic. It might be helpful to write your question out. For example:

> What were the notable philosophies or theories regarding prison reform in 19th century America?

With your topic or question written out, you can identify the key concepts. It is generally best to limit the number of key concepts to two or three. In this particular case, the key ideas would be:

| prison reform | 19th century | America |

Now, consider what synonymous terms or phrases might be used for the ideas you've selected. In addition to synonyms, are there any alternate spellings to your key concepts? Add these additional terms below their respective headings:

prison reform	19th century	America
prison conditions	nineteenth century	United States
penal system	1900's	U.S.

Now you can select your initial search terms from the words and phrases above. There is no need to try to incorporate *all* of the above search terms . Instead, simply select the term or phrase from each column that you think is the most commonly used. After looking through the results of the first search, you may or may not wish to adjust your search terms accordingly. It is important to keep in mind that Internet searching is *not* an exact science and that you should anticipate revising your search terms several times as you go through the search process.

> **HINT:** If, after entering your initial search terms, you get more results than you could possibly look through, you should add another search term or focus your existing terms (make them more specific).
>
> On the other hand, if you get too few results, then you might want to consider eliminating one of your search terms, thereby broadening your search.

Search for phrases using quotation marks

> **HINT:** Phrase searching is ideal if you are looking for a well-known quote. For example, if you type in the phrase "let freedom ring from the prodigious hilltops of New Hampshire," the majority of your results will include a full transcript or excerpts of Martin Luther King's "I Have a Dream" speech.

When searching for a phrase, it is necessary to let the search engine know that you are looking for two or more words *grouped together*. Without such instruction, many search engines will retrieve documents that include the individual words separately, not together as a phrase.

For example, if we simply type in the words *Iowa River* in AltaVista, our results will not necessarily include the phrase *Iowa River*, but instead might merely contain the separate words *iowa* and *river*. Look at the first item that AltaVista retrieved in response to such a search:

AltaVista found 155,678 results About

Iowa Tourism Office
... in the land between the Mississippi **River** and the Missouri **River**, nearly everything you need to know about **Iowa** attractions, destinations special events is just a mouse click away. The **Iowa** ...
www.traveliowa.com • Refreshed in past 48 hours • Related Pages
More pages from www.traveliowa.com

As you can see, this result is not about the Iowa River. Instead, it merely contains the two search terms within the same sentence.

To ensure that AltaVista does search for the words Iowa and River *adjacent to one another*, we need to put quotation marks around the phrase: "Iowa River"

The same will hold true for our search on "prisoner reform" or "criminal reform." Quotation marks must be placed around these phrases to indicate that the terms need to be searched for together.

Example:

Truncation

Truncation is a useful tool if you're searching for multiple variations of a term. When placed at the end of a root word, a truncation symbol represents or replaces all possible endings, thereby searching for variant forms of that term.

For example, if you wish to find biographical information on an individual, you might want to truncate the root term *biog*. Doing so will retrieve results that include the words biography, biographies, biographical, or biographer.

> **WARNING:** While most search engines allow you to truncate, Google is the exception. You cannot truncate search terms within Google!

Most of the major search engines use an asterisk (*) as their truncation symbol. Other common truncation symbols are the exclamation point (!), plus sign (+), and question mark (?). To find out which symbol to use in a specific search engine, consult that search engine's "Help" or "How To" page.

Grinnell College

Limiting Searches by Domain

It can be useful to limit your searches by domain. Domain suffixes (also known as "top-level domains" or "TLD's") indicate what type of group or organization is responsible for hosting an individual web site. Here's a partial list of some of the more common suffixes along with a brief summary of their meaning:

.com   Indicates a "commercial" site. This is the most common top-level domain. Keep in mind that sites ending in ".com" are generally created and maintained by for-profit enterprises.

.org   Indicates "organization." This top-level domain was originally intended for nonprofit groups. Now, however, just about any group can sign up for a .org address.

.gov   Used for federal government sites.

.edu   Indicates an educational institution. This domain suffix applies only to American colleges and universities.

.mil   Any of the U.S. military branches.

.net   Originally reserved for network services providers.

.us   United States. This is a "country-code" top-level domain. For a full list of all country codes, go to http://www.iana.org/cctld/cctld-whois.htm .

.ia.us Indicates a site supported by the state government of Iowa. This includes state offices and public schools.

.uk   Country-code for the United Kingdom

.ac.uk   ".ac" stands for "Academic". The coupling of .ac with .uk denotes an academic institution in the United Kingdom.

.museum One of the newer TLD's. Reserved for museums, museum organizations, and individual members of the museum profession.

If you are searching for information that is likely to be found in just one of these domain types, then you can limit your search accordingly. For example, in Google, select "Advanced Search" from the initial search screen. See the Advanced Search screen image below:

In the **Domain** field, type in the suffix to which you'd like to focus your search. Or, if you wish to search across a number of domains, but want to *exclude* one particular domain type, then you can use the drop-down box to change the "Only" default to "Don't". This allows you to search across all domains types with the exception of the domain suffix you enter in the corresponding search field.

> **HINT:** You can also use this feature to limit your search to a specific server. For example, if you type **grinnell.edu** in the Domain search field, you can limit your search to the pages housed on the www.grinnell.edu server.

Advanced Search Features

Nearly all search engines offer some type of "advanced search" screen. Generally, the advanced search options allow you to control the date range searched, the languages searched, the number of results per page, etc. If you wish to conduct a more precise search, it's always worthwhile to explore the advanced search features.

Boolean Operators

Most search engines support Boolean searching. By employing the Boolean operators AND, OR, NOT in your search statements, you can better describe the relationship between your search terms, which will result in more accurate searches. For more information on Boolean Operators and their use, go to Burling Library's Creating Search Statements instruction guide.

Help Screens

Bear in mind that search engines are forever being updated or revised. This means that these search rules are subject to change. It's *always* a good idea to acquaint yourself with the **Help** or **How To** pages.

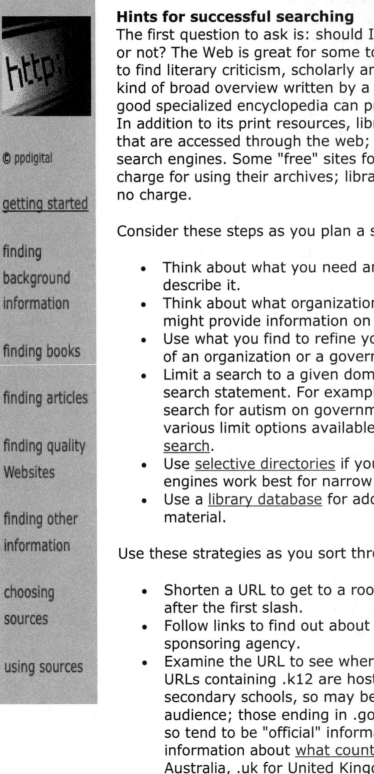

GUSTAVUS FOLKE BERNADOTTE MEMORIAL LIBRARY
GUSTAVUS ADOLPHUS COLLEGE

© ppdigital

getting started

finding
background
information

finding books

finding articles

finding quality
Websites

finding other
information

choosing
sources

using sources

Hints for successful searching

The first question to ask is: should I use the Web for this project or not? The Web is great for some topics, but is not a good place to find literary criticism, scholarly analysis of social issues, or the kind of broad overview written by a noted scholar that a really good specialized encyclopedia can provide.

In addition to its print resources, libraries often pay for resources that are accessed through the web; these aren't indexed in search engines. Some "free" sites for magazines and newspapers charge for using their archives; library databases offer them at no charge.

Consider these steps as you plan a search:

- Think about what you need and which key words might describe it.
- Think about what organizations or government entities might provide information on your topic.
- Use what you find to refine your search (such as the name of an organization or a government agency).
- Limit a search to a given domain by including it in your search statement. For example, **autism site:.gov** will search for autism on government Websites. Or use the various limit options available through an advanced search.
- Use selective directories if you have a broad topic. (Search engines work best for narrow topics or specific facts.)
- Use a library database for additional, high-quality material.

Use these strategies as you sort through your results:

- Shorten a URL to get to a root page by deleting everything after the first slash.
- Follow links to find out about the page's author or sponsoring agency.
- Examine the URL to see where it originated. For example, URLs containing .k12 are hosted at elementary and secondary schools, so may be intended for a young audience; those ending in .gov are government agencies, so tend to be "official" information. Domains may include information about what country the site is from: .au for Australia, .uk for United Kingdom, and so on.

Because there is such a wide variety of information from so many sources on the Web, it's extremely important to evaluate what you find using the same criteria you use for all your sources.

Ironically, Web sources that seem scholarly are quite often badly out of date. The Catholic Encyclopedia, for example, is a copy of a reference work pubished a hundred years ago. The library has the up-to-date 2002 edition in the reference collection, but had to pay rather a lot of money for it. The one that is free online is so old it's no longer under copyright. Unfortunately, though convenient, it's only useful if you want information about the Catholic church in 1907. A few things have changed since then.

Good sites for research

The following are useful for a wide variety of purposes.

Selective directories
Infomine - searchable directory of scholarly sources from the University of California
Librarians' Internet Index - annotated directory of interesting sites
Scirus - a search engine of articles and Web sites in the sciences
Scout Archives - maintained at the University of Wisconsin

Digital archives
American Memory - incredible digital collections from the Library of Congress
Avalon Project - primary documents on US diplomatic history
Electronic Text Center - digital books from the University of Virginia
Eurodocs - European primary documents

News sources
Google News - an automated news aggregator, interesting for English-language world reactions and breaking news
Kidon Media-Link - based in the Netherlands, a directory of worldwide news sources
NewsLink - a US-based news directory
The Big Project - a UK site for international perspectives
Technorati - a blog search tool

Images
Flickr Creative Commons - millions of searchable, copyrighted photos that can be reused under stated conditions.
Google Images - a search engine for image files. The copyright status of these photos is not generally obvious.
MorgueFile - a collection of free images for creative use.
World Images Kiosk - over 50,000 fine art images available for educational use from the California State University system.

Research
Google Scholar - attempts to index and link citations to scholarly work, primarily in the sciences; some of it is not full text, but includes links to text in our library's databases when available. There's also a great deal of information available on the Web in the way of statistics, maps, and official documents. And each of the Web pages for majors includes recommend sites relevant to particular disciplines.

What about Wikipedia?

Many students turn to Wikipedia for background information because it's easy to use, it's vast, and it has become so popular its articles often turn up within the first few links of a Web search. For some topics, particularly in the realm of popular culture, the articles can be valuable. However, there are two things to bear in mind.

First, because authorship is not limited to experts, but is open to anyone, there are times the articles are written by enthusiastic but ignorant amateurs.

Second, because the articles can be changed by anyone, controversial articles are often altered to reflect a paricular perspective, whether for political or PR purposes, and there is a certain amount of vandalism. For an example, see the article on "wiki vandalism."

In general, Wikipedia may be helpul if you're checking something that is "common knowledge" (facts available in multiple sources, such as dates and well-known historical events), or if you are looking for very current information about a topic in contemporary culture that isn't covered elsewhere.

However, it is not generally considered a solid source for most college-level research. Even its founder, Jimmy Wales, cautions students against using Wikipedia for research papers. He told a reporter, "If you are reading a novel that mentions the Battle of the Bulge, for instance, you could use Wikipedia to get a quick basic overview of the historical event to understand the context. But students writing a paper about the battle should hit the history books." The prestigious science journal, *Nature*, caused a stir when it published an analysis that claimed science articles in Wikipedia contained an average of four mistakes, whereas the *Encylopaedia Britannica* contained three - something *Britannica* hotly denied. Nevertheless, for college research you should go beyond general encyclopedias, whether online or in print. If you'd like to know more about Wikipedia, check out interesting, in-depth articles published in The New Yorker and The Atlantic. Or for a politically-barbed, satirical take, see how it was covered by The Colbert Report.

Tips to Effective Internet Searching

Simple Keys To Search the Internet More Effectively:

1. Read the Help or Tips Menu

- Know your Search Tool. What is the difference between a search directory and a search engine? The Help or Tips Menu will provide valuable information about how to perform an effective search. If you have not looked at Help, Tips, or other guides, you are probably not making the best use of the search tool.

2. Prepare to Search

- Think about what you are looking for. Create a list of search terms that you can work with. Consider what is the best search tool for the job. Again, know your search tool--which one will find what you are looking. Do you want to use a search engine like Alta Vista or would you rather use a directory like Yahoo?
  - Table Matching What Your Search May Need with Search Tool Features

3. Start Simple and Take Advantage of the Search Tool

- When you begin a search, use the simple mode to enter search terms.
- Some of the major tools like Alta Vista, AskJeeves, and others have designed the simple mode for ease of use. Natural language searching, links to RealName and DirectHit for finding major sites, and other features like Lycos' First and Fast retrieve good results with minimal expertise. Although the advanced modes offers more control, the simple mode often offers an better results when beginning a search.
- Refrain from entering a search with + and -, Boolean *and*, *or*, and *not*, parenthetical expressions such as *Cleveland and (Indians or Tribe)*, and other advanced features before you have simply entered the search term or terms. If you are searching a phrase, however, the " " around the search will generally lead to better results (see #10).

4. Use Both the Advanced and the Simple Modes of Search Tools

- A common misconception is that Advanced Search is for "advanced searchers." However, the information that you are looking for often dictates how you will search. Learning to work with the Advanced Search modes does not take much more time or energy to learn to use, and it allows you to work with more search options and retrieve sites that are more relevant.

5. Use Unique Terms When Possible to Retrieve More Specific Results

- Search tools use language to retrieve results. The words you choose will determine the information you find. Since some terms generally have one or more meanings, less than perfect results are common when searching the internet. Try to use words that are specific and describe what you are looking for in unique ways. The "Clustering" or "Folders" feature in search tools such as Teoma, WiseNut, and All the Web and the "Refine" feature in Alta Vista can provide other terms to use when searching.

6. Use the Directories in Search Tools or Subject Directories

- Directories, such as what is used by Yahoo, are available on most search tools and help organize sites into categories. Use these categories to focus your search. These search tool directories differ from the "guru" subject directories sites such as Digital Librarian and INFOMINE which list sites that are hand-picked by an individual or groups of individuals who maintain the site.

7. Use More than One Search Tools

- Not all search tools are alike. A search will produce radically different results depending upon the tool used. Each tool has strengths and weaknesses. Take advantage of the strengths and use tools to your advantage. If you want to see this in action, try doing the same search on different tools. Compare the first ten sites retrieved by each tool. Viva la differance!

8. Use the MetaSearch Tools and Natural Language Tools to Begin and/or Refine a Search

- MetaSearch tools, such as Ixquick Metasearch, Vivísimo, ProFusion, SurfWax, and others, search multiple tools simultaneously and are good tools to begin your research. Although the results are rarely as good as using an individual search tool, metasearchers are an excellent way to explore a topic and gather keywords and other information. After using a MetaSearch tool, refine the search by using the available features specific to each individual search tools.
- Natural language searching, available on many tools such as AskJeeves, Alta Vista, and others allows a search to be formulated into a question. Translating a search into a question often helps to you refine the type of information you want to retrieve.

9. Use Capitalization When Appropriate or to Refine a Search

- Not every search tool is case sensitive. However, you will not be penalized by using capitalization for a search such as "Martin Luther King" or "Southern Oregon University Library." Capitalization will often retrieve sites that have the search term in the title--this tactic is especially useful when searching for a terms that are not capitalized unless they are in a title (eg. Computers rather than computers).

10. Use Quotations or Other Symbols to Specify a Phrase

- Search tools do not know whether a search is for "lesson" or "plans." The default is typically lesson or plans in simple searching. Use quotations to surround a phrase such as "lesson plans." However, again a word of caution, when using simple modes in some databases like <u>Alta Vista</u>, searching with quotation will often produce less effective results.

11. Keep Wading to a Minimum: Size of the Search Tool Does Not Matter

- If you have not found what you are looking for in the first 20 to 50 sites, give it up and go no further. Either reformulate your search or try another search tool. Creativity is often the key to reformulating or rephrasing a search.
- The discussion of how many pages are indexed in any particular search tools is generally discussed and in dispute. For the most part, this discussion is a moot point other than when trying to choose a tool for two reasons:
  - No one search engine is best. A sophisticated search requires many search tools.
  - The number of relevant sites is more important than the number of sites searched.

12. Use Find or Ctrl-F to Help Navigate Search Results

- Often it is difficult to understand why a site is retrieved in a search. The Find or Ctrl-F feature will quickly allow you to search the text of a site and locate specific keywords.

Part One: Search Engines

You can use both the **public web** and the **private web** to find information on a topic. A good way to search for information is the Advanced Search feature available in most search engines. Go to http://www.google.com and click on Advanced Search.

Here are a few questions to help you use this resource. Each question is a separate search! Clear the search screen each time.

Using the advanced search function, how do you:

1. Find websites with the exact phrase *Cincinnati Bengals*?

2. Find information about *cancer*, limiting your search to only government web pages?

3. Find web pages that have either the word *teenagers* or the word *adolescents*?

4. Find pages with both of the words *sports* and *drugs*, but not the word *steroids*?

CONCEPTS TO KNOW

Keyword - A term that is important to your topic, or defines/describes your topic. You can search for information using keywords.

Search Engine - A web-based tool that finds other websites based on user input

Database - A collection of information that has been organized in some way

AND - A connecting word or "Boolean Operator" which tells a database to find *both* of the words it links

OR - A connecting word or "Boolean Operator" which tells a database to find *either* of the words it links

>> **Timeline** : Paper Due: 58 days 4 hours | >> **Login** | >> **New Project** | >> **Show All Projects** | >> **Exit**

Research: Find Web Sites

In order to find more scholarly material on the web try these search techniques:

Advanced Googling

Did you know that Google and other search engines have an advanced search page that allows you to have greater control over where you are searching? You can use the advanced search page to be more specific with your search:

- Limit to a particular type of web site, like (.edu, .com, .org, .gov):
  If you are finding too many web pages from commercial sources, you can limit your search to pages that come from an educational institution by typing .edu as a search limit.
- Date updated: You can search for pages updated within a certain range of time.
- Location: Many search engines allow you to find web pages published in a particular country.
- If you are researching current political events, or are looking for information on issues the government may be concerned with, try Google: U.S. Government Search to search state and federal government web sites.

Use Search Techniques to Focus Your Search

Use more words

When you search the web, a one-word or two-word search will often find hundreds of thousands of web sites. To narrow your search and find more relevant web sites, think about your topic and how people might be writing about it. Then use at least three or four keywords or concepts in your search. Instead of searching for acid rain, search for acid rain damage water supply

Search for phrases

If you can describe your topic with words that could also be used as a phrase, narrow your search by enclosing your phrase in quotations. If you don't put your phrases within quotation marks, often the search engine will interpret your search by putting an automatic AND search operator in between your words. So if you type campaign finance disclosures into a search engine, it will be searched like this: campaign AND finance AND disclosures. This might bring up irrelevant results, if the word campaign appears in one paragraph and the word finance appears several paragraphs later.

Example phrase searches: "nixon meets elvis"
                          "nuclear non-proliferation treaty"

You can also use quotation marks to force the search engine to look for commonly used words that might otherwise be left out of your search results. A search engine often ignores words like a, and, and the. If you wanted to find information on the musical **Into The Woods**, you would have better search results by typing *"into the woods"*.

Use search engine math

Many search engines allow you to use the plus sign (+) to require that a word be found on your search results. You can also use a minus sign (-) to exclude words from your search:

+"japanese american internment" –reparations

2004 - 2008 Tufts University

Internet

Search Statements

BOOLEAN OPERATORS FOR INTERNET SEARCHING

AND is understood and is not typed.

OR Forget about the OR

NOT A minus "-" sign replaces this.

An Internet search statement such as this...

global warming north america

...is interpreted as this...

global AND **warming** AND **north** AND **america**

To get these results more accurately, enclose the key phrases in <u>quotes.</u>

"global warming" "north america"

The computer will search for the exact phrase "global warming" and combine it with the exact phrase "north america" giving more accurate results.

Search statement in Google	# of Results
Global warming North America	9,880,000
"Global warming" "North America"	2,350,000

In the first statement, the computer is looking for Global AND warming AND North AND America. In the second statement with the phrases in quotes the computer searches for "Global warming" AND "North America" and delivers fewer and more accurate results.

Narrow it Down

Terms used in Google	# of Results
"Global warming" "North America"	2,350,000
"Global warming" "North America" water	1,710,000

If you wish to add <u>*water*</u> to your search, put it at the end. The AND is implied. See how that narrows down the number of results?

Search the Internet - NOT

Terms used in Google	# of Results
"Global warming" "North America" water	1,710,000
"Global warming" "North America" water –lake	998,000

If you wish to *exclude* water from lakes, just use a **minus sign** and *lake*.

More Examples

Terms used in Google	# of Results	
Social policy	222,000,000	
Social policy health care	66,500,000	
"Social policy" "health care"	1,670,000	
"Social policy" "health care" "United States"	879,000	
"Social policy" "health care" "United States" –California	597,000	NOT

Terms used in Google	# of Results
Social policy	222,000,000
Social policy health care	66,500,000
"Social policy" "health care"	1,670,000
"Social policy" "health care" "United States"	879,000

Which web search will give the fewest results?

- Capital punishment United States
- "Capital punishment" United States
- "Capital punishment" "United States"

Click the box of the appropriate answer

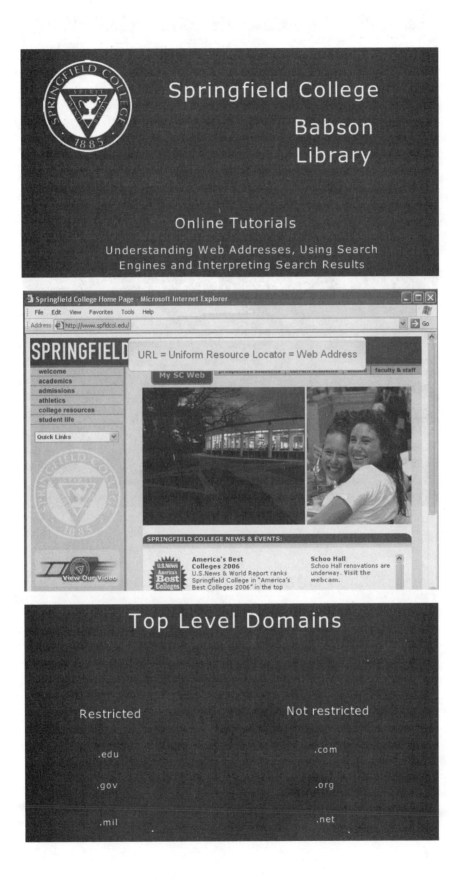

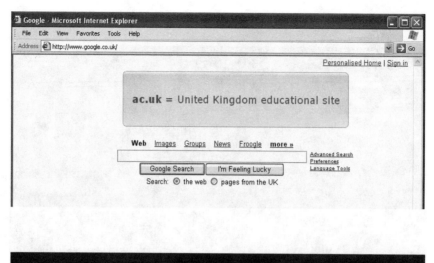

Types of Pages

Text-based	Images
.html / .htm	.jpg
.pdf	.gif
	.png

Search Engines

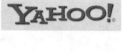

Each search engine returns different results...

because each search engine crawls only a portion of the World Wide Web.

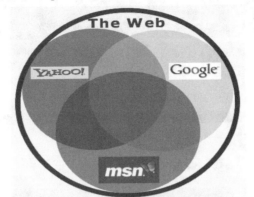

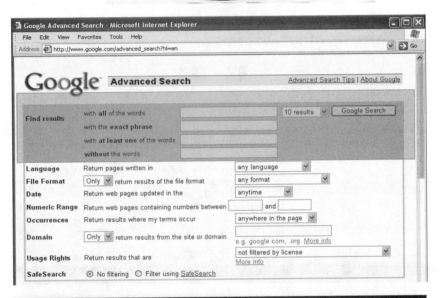

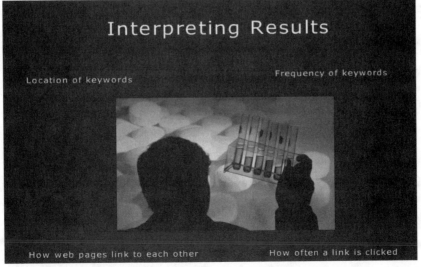

DUGGAN LIBRARY INSTRUCTIONAL SCREENCASTS

10 Tips for Better Google Searching

#1: Phrase Searching

The single most powerful tool in web searching (Google or otherwise) is...

" "

Phrase searching works best with the "discriminating phrase" – the phrase that in common or technical vocabulary describes the concept you are searching.

"affirmative action"
"nuclear proliferation"
"family bed"
"antibiotic resistant bacteria"

#2: Words the Way You Want Them

- Words are automatically STEMMED
search **kite flying** and get matches on **kite, kites, kiting** and **flying, fly, flies**... turn it off with + or " "

+kite +flying or **"kite flying"**

- STOP WORDS are automatically ignored
the, in, a, and, of... etc.
turn off with + or " "

snake +in +the grass
"snake in the grass"

#3: Word Order Matters!

Google's RANKING algorithm favors pages with your terms

❖ in PHRASES
❖ CLOSE TOGETHER
❖ IN THE ORDER TYPED

grass snake
snake grass
snake in the grass
snake +in +the grass
"snake in the grass"

all retrieve different result sets

#4: OR Searching

OR searching requires capitalized OR
   can be used between single words or phrases enclosed in quotes

california OR oregon OR "pacific coast"

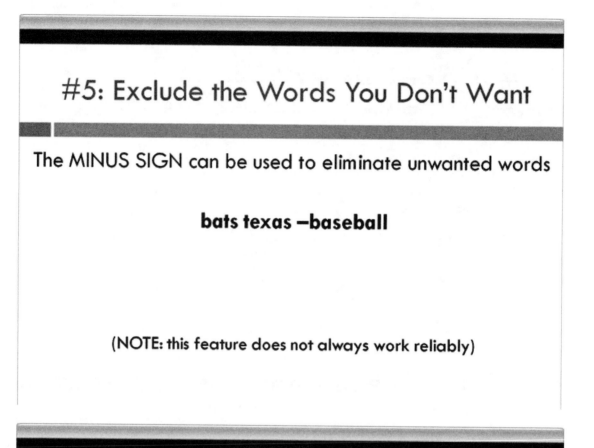

#5: Exclude the Words You Don't Want

The MINUS SIGN can be used to eliminate unwanted words

bats texas −baseball

(NOTE: this feature does not always work reliably)

#6: Punctuation Matters!

Apostrophe ('): **peoples, people's** and **peoples'** are searched as DIFFERENT words

Hypen (-): **same-sex** retrieves *same-sex, same sex,* and *samesex*

Asterix (*): whole word wild card. **george**bush** retrieves *George Bush, George W. Bush, George H.W. Bush, George Herbert Walker Bush...*

#7: Number Ranges

NUMBER RANGE (number..number)
example: find pages mentioning Babe Ruth between 1921 and 1935.

"babe ruth" 1921..1935

#8: Set Limits

Require terms to occur in specific parts of the page or get pages from specific domains.

- ❖ **intitle:** words must appear in <title> field of page
- ❖ **site:** limit to a particular site or type of domain

site:gov retrieves *only* U.S. federal government sites
-site:com retrieves sites from .edu, .gov, .mil, .org, etc. *but NOT .com*

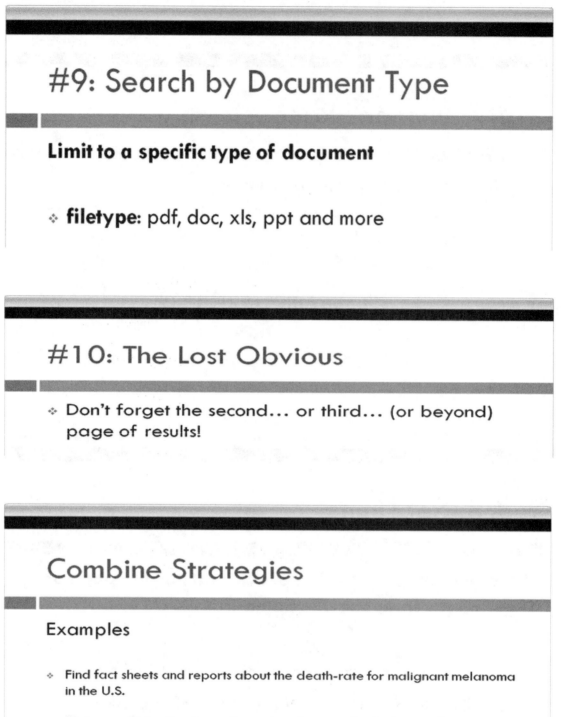

#9: Search by Document Type

Limit to a specific type of document

❖ **filetype:** pdf, doc, xls, ppt and more

#10: The Lost Obvious

❖ Don't forget the second... or third... (or beyond) page of results!

Combine Strategies

Examples

❖ Find fact sheets and reports about the death-rate for malignant melanoma in the U.S.

filetype:pdf death-rate malignant melanoma "united states"

❖ Find PowerPoint presentations from reputable universities in the U.S. about the impact in China of its one-child policy

filetype:ppt site:edu china one-child policy

Web Resource Guides

Facts and Statistics Sources

The purpose of this page is to lead you to **facts and statistics** -- short answers rather than books or journal articles -- and to **unique formats or content**.

The list of sources in each category is intended to be **highly selective** and to provide direct links to a few frequently used fact and statistics sources accessible online. Many are free, credible sites on the open web; others are databases with specialized content to which we subscribe for DSU students, staff and faculty.

Many additional similar sources (online & in print) are available and can be found by searching the Library Catalog and/or asking a librarian for assistance.

Links to Categories of Sources

For access to **more reference sources**, use Excellent Sites for More Reference Sources.

A	D	I	Q
Acronyms & Abbreviations	**Dakota State**	**International /**	**Quotations**
Almanacs	**University**	**Countries**	**R**
Associations/Organizations	**Dictionaries &**	**Internet**	**Research**
Astronomy	**Thesauri**	**L**	**Methods**
Atlases	**Directories**	**Laws &**	**Reviews**
C	**E**	**Legislation**	**S**
Calculators & Converters	**Economics**	**Literary**	**Science &**
Calendars & Holidays	**Encyclopedias**	**M**	**Technology**
Careers & Job-seeking	**English usage**	**Maps**	**September 11**
Cartoons	**Environment**	**Medical**	**South Dakota**
Censorship	**F**	**Information**	**Speeches**
College Catalogs	**Finance - SEE**	**Movies**	**Statistics**
Consumers	**Stocks**	**N**	**Stocks**
Copyright	**G**	**Names**	**T**
Countries / International	**Genealogy**	**Native**	**Taxes**
Current Issues/Hot Topics	**Government**	**American**	**Test Prep**
	Grants	**Sources**	**TV shows**
	Grammar	**P**	**W**
	H	**Patents &**	**Weather**
	Historical	**Trademarks**	**Weights &**
	documents	**Poetry**	**Measures**
	How	**Indexes**	

Excellent Sites for More Reference Sources
"We highly recommend these reference sites!"
Internet Public Library Ready Reference Collection
Virtual Reference Shelf (Library of Congress)
DeskRef, Ramapo Catskill Library System
Infomine General Reference Sources
Librarian's Index to the Internet (LII) Reference Topics

Karl E. Mundt Library & Learning Commons | Dakota State University | Madison, SD

University of Colorado at Colorado Springs

Primary Resources on the Web

Primary documents once available only in print and microfilm collections are available in a digitized format on the World Wide Web from free websites or through subscription services. As with all information on the Web, users must evaluate the authenticity of these documents. Educational and government resources are often more reliable than personal websites. For more information about selecting primary source web sites, go to <u>Using Primary Resources on the Web</u>. Below are some examples of reputable major collections of primary resources, subject directories, and search engines that will help you find primary resource material.

Major Collections and Subject Directories

<u>American Memory</u>

American Memory provides free and open access through the Internet to written and spoken words, sound recordings, still and moving images, prints, maps, and sheet music that document the American experience. It is a digital record of American history and creativity. These materials, from the collections of the Library of Congress and other institutions, chronicle historical events, people, places, and ideas that continue to shape America, serving the public as a resource for education and lifelong learning.

<u>Avalon Project</u>

The Avalon Project, hosted by the Yale Law School containing digitized primary resource material relevant to the fields of Law, History, Economics, Politics, Diplomacy and Government.

<u>Making of America</u>

Making of America is a digital library of primary sources in American social history from the antebellum period through reconstruction. The collection is particularly strong in the subject areas of education, psychology, American history, sociology, religion, and science and technology. It is hosted by the University of Michigan and made possible by a grant from the Andrew W. Mellon Foundation.

<u>Eurodocs</u>

Western European historical documents.

<u>National Archives and Records Administration</u>

NARA includes the major documents of our government, the Declaration of Independence, the Constitution of the United States, and the Bill of Rights, as well as the 100 milestone documents of American history.

<u>National Security Archives</u>

A library and archive of declassified U.S. documents obtained through the Freedom of Information Act.

<u>History Matters</u>

History Matters contains more than 800 reviewed and annotated web site in American History.

<u>History Guide</u>

History Guide is a subject gateway to scholarly relevant websites in history.

© University of Colorado at Colorado Springs

RESEARCH GUIDES
Examples of Online Historical Primary Sources

Library Primary Source Databases

Historical New York Times
Search and browse the New York Times from 1851 until 2003.

Early American Newspapers
Over 700 early U.S. newspapers from 1690-1876 full text and searchable.

Internet Resources for Primary Sources

American Memory from the Library of Congress
American Memory provides free and open access through the Internet to written and spoken words, sound recordings, still and moving images, prints, maps, and sheet music that document the American experience. It is a digital record of American history and creativity.

Army Heritage Collection Online
Search of browse the Army Heritage and Education Center's on-line resources.

Avalon Project at Yale Law School
The Avalon Project is dedicated to providing access via the World Wide Web to primary source materials in the fields of Law, History, Economics, Politics, Diplomacy and Government.

CIA FOIA Reading Room
View formerly classified documents made public under Freedom of Information Act requests.

Civil Rights in Mississippi Digital Archive
Collection of photos, documents, and oral histories from the University of Southern Mississippi Libraries.

Documenting the American South
Primary resources for the study of Southern literature, history and culture.

Eisenhower Presidential Library Primary Sources
Excellent display of primary sources from events of the Eisenhower era.

Flickr Commons
Find historical photos placed online by cultural heritage institutions.

Making of America
A digital library of primary sources in American social history from the antebellum period through reconstruction.

National Security Archive
An independent non-governmental research institute and library located at The George Washington University, the Archive collects and publishes declassified documents obtained through the Freedom of Information Act.

New York Public Library Digital Gallery
Over 600,000 images digitized from primary sources and printed rarities in the collections of The New York Public Library, including illuminated manuscripts, historical maps, vintage posters, rare prints and photographs, illustrated books, printed ephemera, and more.

United States Military Academy Library Digital Collections
Manuscripts, maps, photographs and multimedia from the US Military Academy at West Point.

Vietnam Center and Archive
The mission of the Vietnam Archive at Texas Tech University is to support and encourage research and education regarding all aspects of the American Vietnam experience; promoting a greater understanding of this experience and the peoples and cultures of Southeast Asia.

RESEARCH GUIDES

Finding Web Resources in History

Introduction

Some people may tell you that you can't find quality resources on the Web. For most subject areas, this is simply not true. The Web can be a treasure trove of quality information; the problem is that you have to sift through the trillions of pages that are not quality. And you need to be able to tell the difference.

Here are just some of the places you can find quality resources on the Web.

- **Scholarly repositories** - like the University of California's eScholarship Repository

- **Digital Archives** - like Civil War Women and American Memory
- **University institutes and initiatives** - like The Avalon Project at Yale Law School and The Vietnam Center and Archive at Texas Tech

- **Government Websites** - like the National Archives and the Central Intelligence Agency

- **Reputable think-tanks** - like the Woodrow Wilson International Center for Scholars

- **Presidential libraries** - like the Eisenhower Library or the FDR Library

Tricks of the Trade

Many libraries, institutes and researchers have created bibliographies and research guides on specific subjects.

- Search for your topic with the word bibliography.
  - Example: World War II Bibliography.
- Search for your topic keyword and add "guide" or "web guide" or "subject guide".
  - Example: Soviet History Guide
  - Example: Medieval History Subject Guide.

Look in particular for resources from .edu and .gov sites, though there may be some reputable sources from .org's or even .com's.

In Google's advanced search interface, you can limit your search to specific domains (.edu, .gov, etc.). You can also limit your search to file formats like .doc and .pdf which will make it more likely that you'll find a research paper in the bunch. Be careful of research papers: something from a scholar with their doctorate or a Masters Thesis can be cited; something written by a college or high school student can not.

A number of major research libraries are working with Google to digitize their books and make those in the public domain (pre-1923) freely available online. Another group of libraries and related institutions are doing the same with the Internet Archive. There are a number of other institutions that have been digitizing books in the public domain for years. These can usually be read online or even downloaded to your computer.

RESEARCH GUIDES

How to Find Online Books

eBooks in Our Collection

The library has tens of thousands of eBooks in our collection. All of them can be found in the library catalog. The majority of our eBooks come from eBrary though we have a few in NetLibrary as well. We also subscribe to a collection of reference books (dictionaries and encyclopedias) called Credo Reference that allows you to search within a specific book, across a handful of topically related books, or across the entire Credo collection.

Free eBook Repositories Online

- Google Books - Google is digitizing books from the major libraries of the world (Stanford, New York Public Library, Harvard, and the British Library, to name a few). They are making all of the works they digitize that are outside of copyright -- mainly those before 1923, with some exceptions -- available online to be read or downloaded. When you do a search, you will find results that you can read in full and ones that are protected by copyright. If you click on **Full view** at the top of the results list, you will only get results that you can read in full and download.
- Internet Archive - The Internet Archive is working with another group of universities to digitize works in the public domain. They have an interesting format called flip book where you can actually turn the pages of the eBook like a normal book.
- Project Gutenberg - The oldest free eBook site. Includes works from the classical era into the 1900s. Includes many primary sources and reference works.
- Perseus Digital Library - large digital library of primary source works in history, science, and the humanities.
- The Online Books Page - site at the University of Pennsylvania that allows users to search multiple eBooks sites at once (including Perseus and Gutenberg).
- Bartelby - includes reference works and American and British poetry, fiction and essays.
- Combined Arms Research Library Digital Library - includes ebooks from the School of Advanced Military Study, Masters theses, operational documents from various wars and more.
- Many Universities are conducting their own digitization projects. For example, Illinois Harvest includes books digitized from the University of Illinois and the Harvard University Open Collections Program provides digitized books from their archives and special collections. Columbia University Press' Gutenberg-e site allows free access to its collection of award-winning books on history.
- If you're looking for a specific work or works by a specific author, it doesn't hurt to try doing a regular web search for the work or author. The second search result for playwright Eugene O'Neill includes electronic versions of his plays. Obviously, this will only work for writers whose works are in the public domain.

Augustana College
Thomas Tredway Library

U.S. Government Information Resources

This is a guide to websites that provide full-text access to United States government publications and other documents. Most of the links below lead directly to full-text access points, not the home pages of the sponsoring government agencies. Use usa.gov as a portal for finding government websites other than those listed here.

- Major Government Resources
- Resources by Branch of Government
- Resources by Executive Department
- Resources from Independent Executive Agencies
- Artwork, Photographs and Other Images

Major Government Resources:

USA.gov

The primary web portal to information on the United States government. Begin here to find government agencies' websites, or browse for a variety of other types of information provided by the government.

Catalog of U.S. Government Publications (Government Printing Office)

Centralized catalog for accessing a large variety of government publications. Links to full-text are provided where available. For assistance in finding print documents see the CGP's Federal Depository Library Directory.

GPO Access Online Resources: Resource List A-Z or By Branch of Government

A comprehensive list of publications and other resources available in full-text online through the Government Printing Office. Browse by either the alphabetized list of titles, or by branch of government. Years of availability are clearly indicated for each publication. Some highlights from this resource list:

- 9-11 Commission Report
- Congressional Hearings
- Historic Government Publications from World War II
- Historical Publications of the United States Commission on Civil Rights
- Public Papers of the Presidents of the United States
- State of the Union Addresses
- Supreme Court Nomination Hearings

Statistical Abstract of the United States (U.S. Census Bureau)

Statistics on a wide range of social, economic and political topics. These statistics come from a variety of government agencies and private organizations, as well as the most recent United States census. The *Statistical Abstract* is also available in print in the Tredway Library's reference collection: HA202 .S797

Resources by Branch of Government:
Executive Branch:
WhiteHouse.gov

Information on the present administration and its agenda. For addresses, press releases and other statements click "The Briefing Room."
Legislative Branch:

Congressional Research Service Reports (University of North Texas Libraries)
Congressional Research Service Reports (Center for Democracy and Technology)
Reports compiled by the service that conducts research for Congress. There is no single government site that provides complete access to these, but other organizations have developed online collections to make them available. These are two of the more extensive collections.
Government Accountability Office Reports (Government Accountability Office)
GAO reports, some of which date back to the earlier 20th century. Search by full-text or report title. Documents will be available in html and pdf formats.
Library of Congress Digital Collections (Library of Congress)
An easy access point to digitized portions of the Library of Congress's collections, including the American Memory Project. This site is best suited to browsing, as the search box on the top right-hand corner of the page is for the entire Library of Congress website, not just the digital collections.
THOMAS (Library of Congress)
Full-text of various types of legislative documents, including bills, treaties and the Congressional Record. Named after Thomas Jefferson, this service was established in 1995 at the order of the 104th Congress, to increase the public's access to legislative information.
For other Congressional publications, including Congressional Hearings and the Congressional Record, see the GPO Access resource list, above.

Judicial Branch:
Supreme Court Decisions, 1937-1975 (National Technical Information Service)
Full-text of Supreme Court decisions 1937-1975. The top search boxes are for case-name searches; the bottom search boxes are for full-text, keyword searches. The National Technical Information Service, which is part of the Department of Commerce, provides this service through FedWorld, an online project designed to disseminate government information to the public.
Supreme Court Decisions, 1991-present (Supreme Court of the United States)
This site quite simply provides access to pdf versions of bound volumes; it is not readily searchable. A volume can be over 1000 pages, and there is one pdf file for each volume, so files will take some time to open completely; it is advisable to download files before opening them, to avoid encountering a "time-out" problem. The site also warns that, in the case of discrepancies, the print versions of these documents are still considered authoritative. Click "Information About Opinions" on the main page for detailed background on the issuance and dissemination of Supreme Court opinions.

Resources by Executive Department:
AGRICULTURE
--U. S. Forest Service: Treesearch
Full-text of articles on forestry written by U. S. Forest Service scientists. All publications since January 2004 are available here; older publications are in the process of being added, but coverage is not complete.

COMMERCE
--Bureau of the Census: American Factfinder
Fast-facts drawn from the 2000 census. The table of contents, on the left-hand side of the page, leads to categories of census-related, demographic information.
--Bureau of the Census: 2000 Census of Population and Housing
Access point for pdf versions of the 2000 census: begin by narrowing down to a particular section of the document, from which point you can open a pdf of that section. Clicking "Demographic Profile Data Search" leads to a search screen from which you select a state, followed by a particular area within that state, to go immediately to that narrowly-defined portion of the census.

Portions of earlier decennial censuses have also been digitized in an effort to make as much census information as possible readily available to the public.
--U. S. Patent and Trademark Office: Patent Search
Full-text patents 1976-present; page images 1790-1975. The latter are searchable only by patent number, issue date, and current U.S. classifications. Read the Notices and Policies page for further information.

DEFENSE: Publications
A small selection of documents are linked from the main publications page; others are locatable through the search function or document archive, the latter of which is organized alphabetically by document title (see links on the right side of the publications page).
Secretary of Defense Speeches Archive
Beginning January 1995; speeches are organized by date.

EDUCATION
--Institute of Education Sciences: Publications & Products Search
Publications from a variety of sub-agencies of the Department of Education. Search by title, author, subject, organization or type of publication.
--National Center for Education Statistics: Annual Reports
Reports from the organization in charge of education-related data in the United States. Click on a report title to access the most recent version. Browse the tabs on top of the page—"Surveys & Programs," "Tables & Figures," etc.—for additional information compiled by the NCES.

ENERGY: Information Bridge
Department of Energy research reports since 1991. This site is not browsable, but it offers a "Fielded Search" option (by such criteria as author, research organization, sponsoring organization, etc.) in addition to the "Basic Search" on the main page.
--National Renewable Energy Laboratory: NREL Publications
Search interface for publications of the NREL, which specializes in renewable energy and energy-efficient technologies. Publications go back to 1977, and many are available full-text.

HEALTH AND HUMAN SERVICES
--Centers for Disease Control and Prevention: CDC Wonder
Database of CDC reports and statistical data on a wide variety of public health topics. CDC Wonder is both keyword-searchable and browsable. Browsing is available both by subject ("Topics" tab) and by an alphabetical listing of report and dataset titles ("A-Z Index" tab).
--National Library of Medicine & National Institutes of Health: PubMed
Citations to journal articles in medicine going back to the 1950s. Many articles are available in full-text; look for links to full-text by the article's citation. For articles not available in full-text, check "Augustana's Periodicals" to see if we subscribe to the publication. To get the complete title of the journal, open the article abstract by clicking on the author's name; then, point your mouse at the hyperlinked abbreviation of the journal title.

HOMELAND SECURITY: Immigration Statistics
Recent reports on immigration in the United States, including legal and illegal immigration, naturalization, and refugees.

HOUSING AND URBAN DEVELOPMENT: HUD User
Publications and research reports from HUD's Office of Policy Development and Research. See the First Time Visitor Page for specifics on using this site.

INTERIOR
--Bureau of Land Management: General Land Office Records
Records of the sale of U.S. government-owned land. The main feature of this site is the "Land Patent Search": Enter the state and the name of a person who (may have) bought land from the United States government; or, go to the "Standard" search tab and choose "All States" if the location of the sale is unknown. Clicking on the name of the person being searched leads to basic information about the sale. From here, click on the "Document Image" tab, then select a file type, to access a digitized version of the original document. Recently added to the General Land Office Records site are surveys conducted at the time the land was sold; these are still being updated and do not cover all 50 states.

--National Park Service: History
Publications on various topics in national park history, including the founding and administration of parks; prehistory and history prior to parks' founding; and geology, ecology and environmental history, to name just a few. Topics covered vary from park to park. The National Park Service has permission to reproduce all of these documents full-text online, but note that most are still under copyright. In the table of contents on the left-hand side of the page, click "National Park Service History" for information on the NPS as a whole, and "Park Histories" for information on particular national parks.

--National Park Service: National Historic Landmark Theme Studies
Studies conducted to determine or justify the historic value of sites under consideration for National Historic Landmark status. These tend to be completed in consultation with scholars and experts in the area of study. Click here for the NPS's definition of theme studies. To find specific historic landmarks and/or the applications submitted to have sites named landmarks, browse the "Quicklinks" on the National Historic Landmarks webpage.

--United States Geological Survey: Publications Warehouse
Publications—reports, data sets, series, etc.—of the USGS, archived full-text for free online. Conduct a Basic or Advanced search; or, click "Contents" for an overview of the series made available by the USGS.

JUSTICE: Resources or FOIA Reading Rooms
Reports and other DOJ publications, available full-text online for free. On the "Resources" site click "Publications by Agency" for links to online reading rooms--collections of full-text electronic publications--established by sub-agencies of the Department of Justice. The "FOIA Reading Rooms" provide access to electronic records made available specifically through the Freedom of Information Act (FOIA); these may overlap somewhat--but not entirely--with those linked through the "Resources" site.

--Bureau of Alcohol, Tobacco, Firearms and Explosives: Publications
Browsable as opposed to searchable; organized by topic and type of information. The earliest available publications go back to the mid-1990s.

--Federal Bureau of Investigation: Electronic Reading Room
FBI files released under the Freedom of Information Act; the most commonly-requested items have been digitized and made available at this website. The easiest access points are the Electronic Reading Room A-Z list and/or browsing categories.

LABOR: FOIA Reading Room
A list of staff manuals; opinions and orders; policy statements; and other frequently-requested documents from all sub-agencies of the Department of Labor. Organized by type of publication.

--Bureau of Labor Statistics: Office of Publications & Special Studies
Publications from the agency that keeps track of labor-related data in the United States, for use both by the government and by U. S. citizens and residents. Browse by publication type. Or, click on one of the BLS's most popular publications, on the left-hand side of the page; the most

significant of these is the *Occupational Outlook Handbook*, a guide to the current market for various careers and job-types across the United States.

STATE: Secretary's Comments
Transcripts of interviews, remarks and other statements by the Secretary of State. On the left-hand side of the page, click on a year to find remarks by date; or, click "Search Secretary of State Pages" to find remarks by topic or keyword.
--Bureau of Public Affairs: Background Notes
Background/overview information on the countries of the world—basic statistics, demographic information, history, economy, politics and foreign relations—compiled by the regional bureaus of the Department of State. This webpage provides access to the most recent Background Notes on each country, but a link near the top of the page leads to earlier editions.

TREASURY
--Internal Revenue Service: Forms and Publications
For locating, downloading and printing federal tax forms and other tax-related information from the IRS.

TRANSPORTATION: DOT Library: Online Digital Special Collections
Digitized documents from the Department of Transportation. The links on this main page are titles of collections; click on a title to access lists of individual documents within each collection.
-- Nat'l Highway Traffic Safety Admin.: Fatality Analysis Reporting System Encyclopedia
For national data on traffic accidents going back to 1994. The main page provides a general overview. Click "Reports" for more focused break-downs of the data; click "Query" to construct your own report; or click "Publications" to access brochures, fact sheets and other print reports in pdf format.

VETERANS' AFFAIRS: FOIA Reading Room
Brief list of digitized documents from the Department of Veterans' Affairs, mostly reports, policies and other documents on the workings of the department.

Resources from Independent Executive Agencies:
Central Intelligence Agency: FOIA Electronic Reading Room
Access point for declassified CIA documents, many of which are available electronically. The search box is on the top of this page; or, browse featured collections or frequently-requested documents. Click "Publications," in the menu on the left-hand side of the page, for other items, including the CIA *World Factbook*.

Environmental Protection Agency: National Service Center for Environmental Publications
Thousands of Environmental Protection Agency publications, many of which are free and full-text. Use the "Simple," "Field" or "Advanced" search options; browsing is not advisable here, as browsing menus are arranged almost strictly by EPA document number.

National Archives and Records Administration:
Archival Research Catalog
The online catalog for the National Archives and Records Administration. Searches may be limited to only those documents that have been digitized and made available online: click the blue and yellow ARC icon in the middle of this page, then click the "Digital Copies" button on the new window that appears. Also see the Archival Research Catalog Galleries for a quick overview of topics and collections currently being featured by the National Archives.

100 Milestone Documents
One hundred primary documents significant to United States history. Arrangement is strictly chronological.

Access to Archival Databases
Searches electronic records compiled by a variety of government agencies. Records to be made available were determined by their interest value: most address specific people, places and dates and are helpful for research in areas like genealogy and history. "Browse by Category" to get a broad overview of what is available, or select the "Getting Started Guide" for help with finding and using the available information.

Artwork, Photographs and Other Images:
Galaxy of Images (Smithsonian Institution Libraries)
Digital reproductions of images from books owned by the Smithsonian Institution Libraries. Point to "Explore the Collections" on the upper left-hand corner of the page, then select from the searching and browsing options.
National Gallery of Art: The Collection (National Gallery of Art)
Digital images of a significant portion of the National Gallery of Art's collection. On the collection's main webpage, search by a variety of parameters (title, author, subject, provenance, accession number, etc.) or scroll down to browse.
National Park Service Photographs (National Park Service / Harpers Ferry Center)
Over 2000 photographs of national parks, many dating back to the 19th century or early 20th century. Click "Search the Collection" to begin.
NIX: NASA Image eXchange (National Aeronautics and Space Administration)
Photos and images of outer space, as well as goings-on at NASA. Search on the main NIX page; or, browse by subject categories on the right-hand side of the main page.
Smithsonian Photography Initiative (Smithsonian Institution)
A portion of the more than 13 million photographs owned by the Smithsonian Institution. Begin by clicking "Search Images" on the top right-hand corner of the page. Then, conduct a keyword search or browse by topic.

Thomas Tredway Library ■Augustana College ■639 38th Street, Rock Island, IL 61201

Find Government Information

A directory of government information websites.

Indexes to Government Information

Business.gov - Business Gateway, managed by the Small Business Administration and 21 other agencies, to provide access to government services and information for businesses.

Catalog of United States Government Publications - Provides an index to print and electronic publications created by Federal agencies. When available, links are provided to the full-text of these publications.

GPO's Federal Digital System (FDsys) The migration of information from GPO Access into FDsys will be complete in 2010.

Federal Government Agencies Page - Provides links to departments within federal agencies.

FedWorld - Gateway to government information managed by the National Technical Information Service (NTIS).

FindLaw - A bibliography of legal resources on the web including state laws, Supreme Court decisions, and a legal subject index.

Forms from the Feds - Forms for copyright, passports, taxes, savings bonds, and many more.

Google U.S. Government Search - Searches government and news websites. Searches can be limited to government websites.

Government Information Online: Ask a Librarian - Chat or email a question to government information librarians.

Government Printing Office (GPO) Access - Access to information resources published by the Federal Government.

Government Information Xchange - Includes links to state and local government information.

MarciveWeb Docs UCCS only - Index to U.S. government publications from 1976 to the present.

New Electronic Titles - Includes Web-accessible U.S. Government publications of public interest or educational value.

Regulations.gov - All proposed Federal regulations that are open for public comment and rules as published in the Federal Register.

Science.gov - Science.gov searches databases and selected websites containing U.S. government science information, including research and development results.

United States Government Documents (Internet Archive) - Collection of full text historical and current government documents.

U.S. Government Policy and Supporting Positions ("The Plum Book") - The 2008 edition of listing of government positions.

USA.gov (formerly FirstGov) - The U.S. government's official web portal.

Executive Branch and Executive Agencies

The President. The chief executive of the United States. Presidential duties are defined in the Constitution, assigned by the legislature, and based on custom and tradition. These include leadership of the armed forces, diplomatic relations with foreign countries, administration of the executive offices, appointment of officials, and veto of legislation.

- The Executive Office of the President (EOP or EXOP)
- The White House
- Public Papers of the Presidents
- Electronic Code of Federal Regulations

The President's Cabinet. The heads (Secretaries) of executive departments advise the President and oversee the operations of the executive departments.

- Department of Agriculture
- Department of Commerce
    - National Climatic Data Center
        - National Climatic Data Center Online Document Library (**NOTE**: If off campus, you must be on the Library VPN for this link to work)
    - National Oceanic & Atmospheric Administration (NOAA)
- Department of Defense
- Department of Education
    - Doing What Works
- Department of Energy
    - Office of Environmental Management
    - Information Bridge: DOE Scientific and Technical Information (Department of Energy)
- Department of Health and Human Services
    - Center for Disease Control (CDC)
    - Food & Drug Administration (FDA)
    - National Institutes of Health (NIH)
    - Substance Abuse & Mental Health Services Administration (SAMHSA)
- Department of Homeland Security
    - Bureau of Citizenship and Immigration Service (INS)
    - Ready.Gov
- Department of Housing and Urban Development
- Department of the Interior

- o   National Park Service
- o   United States Geological Survey (USGS)
- Department of Justice
  - o   National Criminal Justice Reference Service (NCJRS)
- Department of Labor
  - o   Occupational Safety & Health Administration (OSHA)
- Department of State
  - o   Electronic Archive of Information Released Prior to January 20, 2001
- Department of Transportation
  - o   Federal Aviation Administration (FAA)
  - o   Federal Highway Administration
- Department of the Treasury
- Department of Veterans Affairs

Independent Regulatory Agencies - usually headed by a board or commission and are not under the President's direct control.

- Federal Communications Commission (FCC)

Government Corporations are considered part of the executive branch but operate independently.

- United States Postal Service

Legislative Branch

U.S. Congress. The national legislature of the United States. Consists of two bodies - the Senate (100 members, 2 from each state) and the House of Representatives (435 members, representation based on state population).

- Congressional Pictorial Directory: 110th Congress
- U.S.Senate
- U.S. House of Representatives

Legislation

- THOMAS - legislative information from the Library of Congress
- Legislative branch resources of Government Printing Office (GPO)
- Laws and Regulations - General Reference
- Century of Lawmaking for a New Nation

Library of Congress

- American Memory
- Copyright Office

University of Colorado at Colorado Springs

Judicial Branch

<u>Federal Judiciary</u>. The national system of courts and judges that interpret laws and render judgment.

- <u>The Supreme Court</u>
    - o <u>U.S. Supreme Court Decisions</u>
    - o <u>Selected Historic Decisions of the Supreme Court</u>
    - o <u>Supreme Court Decisions 1937 - 1975</u>
    - o <u>OYEZ: U.S Supreme Court Media (Multimedia Archive)</u>
- <u>U.S. Federal Courts Finder</u>

Colorado State and Local Governments

<u>State of Colorado</u>

- <u>Colorado State Documents Index</u>
- <u>Quick Guide to Colorado State Governmental Statistical Information</u>
- <u>Code of Colorado Regulations</u>
- <u>Colorado Legislative Process</u>
- <u>Colorado Department of Revenue TAX UPDATE</u>

International

Government Links

- <u>Law and Government Resources</u>
- <u>Foreign Government Resources on the Web (University of Michigan)</u>
- <u>Governments on the WWW</u>
- <u>General Foreign Government Resources (University of California, Berkeley, Library)</u>
- <u>Government Information: International (University of California, San Diego, Library)</u>
- <u>National Government Information (United Nations)</u>
- <u>Global Legal Information Network (GLIN)</u>
- <u>Foreign and International Law Guide (Cornell Law School)</u>

Country Information

- <u>Foreign Information by Country (University of Colorado at Boulder)</u>
- <u>International Information (Northwestern University Library)</u>
- <u>The World Factbook (Central Intelligence Agency)</u>
- <u>Background Notes (U.S. Department of State)</u>
- <u>Country Studies and Profiles (Library of Congress)</u>
  "Studies included here were published between 1988 and 1998. Information on some countries may no longer be up to date. See the "Research Completed" date at the beginning of each study or the "Data as of" date at the end of each section of text. <u>United Nations System Pathfinder</u>
- <u>Country Profiles (BBC)</u>   © University of Colorado at Colorado Springs

Hannon Library Home » LibGuides Home » Faculty Services   Admin Sign In

Faculty Services

This pages lists faculty services at the Hannon Library at Southern Oregon University.

Last update: Oct 29th, 2009 | URL: http://libguides.sou.edu/facultyservices | ▤ Print/Mobile Guide | ▨ RSS Updates | ▣ SHARE ◢▨◢

| Home | Online Teaching Sources |

Online Teaching Sources 🗩 Comments (0) ▤ Print/Mobile Page   Search   [This Guide ▾] (Go)

Scholarly Web Sites and Learning Objects

The sources below provide access to a rich collection of online content to supplement and/or replace textbooks. Few of the resources below point to commercial sites.

- MERLOT(Multimedia Educational Resources for Learning and Online Teaching)
  Great resource for online teaching. Browse and search discipline specific collections. To find Learning Objects use Advanced Search and select "simulation" from the "Material Type" pull down menu. Set up a personal account to store all your sites.
- Infomine
  Contains reviewed scholarly web sites in social sciences, humanities, and sciences.
- OAIster: find the pearls
  Provides access to numerous digital archives around the world. Includes text, image, and audio digital collections.
- Registry of Open Access Repository (ROAR)
  A guide to content stored on university Institutional Repositories around the world. Contains article pre-prints and post-prints, datasets, theses and dissertations, and numerous primary source and image collections. Select CONTENT SEARCH button to conduct searches.
- DOAJ: Directory of Open Access Journals
  Over 4,500 open access scholarly journals from around the world.
- Google Scholar
  Provides access to scholarly literature however it does contain commercial book and journal sites and points to Wikipedia.
- Intute
  Similar to Infomine. Good browsing scheme and search capabilities. Seven university libraries in the United Kingdom review the sites.
- Rice Connexions
  "Connexions is an environment for collaboratively developing, freely sharing, and rapidly publishing scholarly content on the Web."
- Wisc-Online
  A Wisconsin site for learning objects.
- Internet Archive
  Provides access to over 350,000 cultural artifacts in digital form. The Archive is divided into 5 Collections including Text, Moving Images, Audio, Web, and Live Music Archive.

Want better results? Search these sites independently.

American Authors (http://guweb2.gonzaga.edu/faculty/campbell/enl311/aufram.html)
A nice site with useful links and information regarding primarily 19th century American authors. Also included is a timeline, literary movements, and external links to other American literature sites.

American Studies@ The University of Virginia
(http://xroads.virginia.edu/~HYPER/hypertex.html)
Access online primary text to American Studies works ranging from Jane Addams (My Twenty Years at Hull House) to WPA American Slave Narratives.

American Verse Project (http://www.hti.umich.edu/a/amverse/)
An electronic archive of volumes of American poetry prior to 1920.

Bartelby.com (http://www.bartleby.com/)
Well-known web publisher of literature (fiction and non-fiction), reference, and verse. All content is free. Hint; scan the Indexes to get an idea of available content.

Catalogue of Digitized Medieval Manuscripts (http://manuscripts.cmrs.ucla.edu)
Search or browse (by location of archive, language, author, title) for fully digitized medieval manuscripts that are freely available on the web.

Complete Works of William Shakespeare (http://the-tech.mit.edu/Shakespeare/)
As the site title provides, access all of the Bard's works online. Includes a link to the "Mr. Shakespeare and the Internet" site for other Shakespeare-related stuff.

Foklore and Mythology Electronic Texts (http://www.pitt.edu/~dash/folktexts.html)
A collection that is international in scope with a rich selection of Nordic/Germanic pieces. Main complaint is the lack of an internal search engine which would be useful since arrangement is a bit haphazard (sometimes by theme, other times by author, location, or culture.

Literary History.com: Changing the Status Quo of Academia
(http://www.literaryhistory.com/)
More than 2,000 high quality literary criticism citations to more than 250 nineteenth and twentieth century writers.

Literary Resources on the Net (http://andromeda.rutgers.edu/~jlynch/Lit/)
This site contains links to English literature pages, although one of the sixteen categories is "Other National Literatures". The page contains a simple search engine (one word entry) to facilitate navigation across the categories. Not particularly well organized, nonetheless, a decent place to begin searching for web sites devoted to specific authors, movements, and collections. Coverage extends from the Classical period to the Twentieth century.

Luminarium (http://www.luminarium.org/lumina.htm)
A handsome web site that provides quality access to Middle English, Renaissance, and 17th century literature. Information about, as well as works by, the included authors are about as comprehensive as one can get on the web.

New Chaucer Society (http://artsci.wustl.edu/~chaucer/links.php)
Links to various Chaucer homepages, E-texts, and bibliography as well as other Medieval sites.

Oxford Text Archive (http://ota.ahds.ac.uk/)
Digital texts of several thousand classic works available for free download, from Leviathan to Paradise Lost and a lot more in between.

Poetry Archive (http://www.poetryarchive.org/poetryarchive/home.do)
A website containing poets reading their own poems. Requires RealPlayer (link to download free version of RealPlayer provided). Want to hear Langston Hughes read, "The Negro Speaks of Rivers"? If so, this is your site.

Project Gutenberg (http://gutenberg.net/)
Free electronic text of books in public domain from this well established site.

Evaluating Web Sites

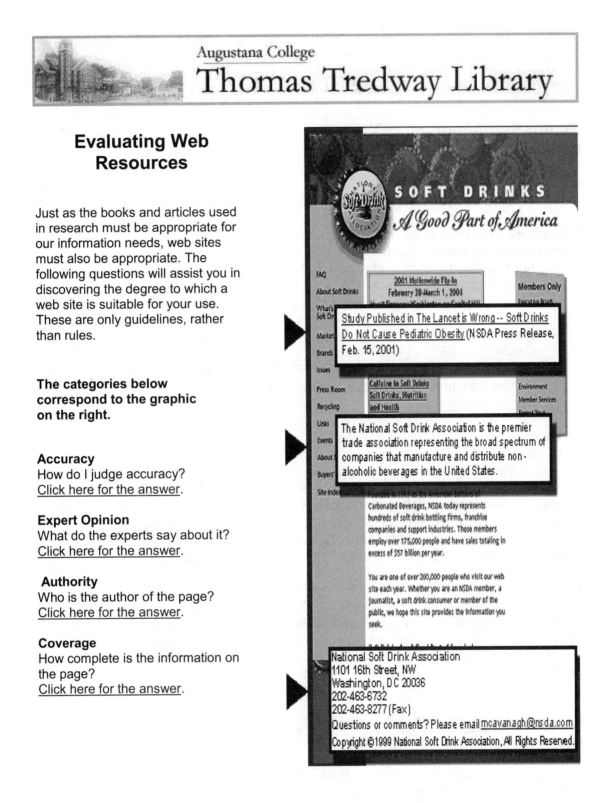

Evaluating Web Resources

Just as the books and articles used in research must be appropriate for our information needs, web sites must also be appropriate. The following questions will assist you in discovering the degree to which a web site is suitable for your use. These are only guidelines, rather than rules.

The categories below correspond to the graphic on the right.

Accuracy
How do I judge accuracy?
Click here for the answer.

Expert Opinion
What do the experts say about it?
Click here for the answer.

Authority
Who is the author of the page?
Click here for the answer.

Coverage
How complete is the information on the page?
Click here for the answer.

Evaluating <u>Accuracy</u> in Web Resources

Questions to ask:
Are the sources of the information listed?
Is this information fact or opinion?
Can the information be verified from an independent source?

Resources to use for answering the questions:
Some independent sources to use for verification:

- For statistics try <u>Statistical Abstracts</u> [also in print: REF HA 202 .S797] or one of the almanacs in reference [REF AY section].
- For biographical information try *Biography and Genealogy Master Index* [REF CT 213 .B56]
- If it is a news story, try one of these full text databases: <u>Lexis/Nexis Academic Universe</u>, or <u>EBSCO Academic Search Elite</u>.
- To see if others share an opinion, try *Editorials on File* [REF D 839 .E3]
- To see if a journal is reputable, peer-reviewed, and/or respected, try <u>Ulrich's Periodicals Directory</u>.

So what?
If the authors of the web page give intellectual credit (a bibliography, if you want to call it that), then they aren't worried about you checking up on their research. Even if they are offering information without citing the origin, if you can verify that information from a source that is independent, it is a vote for the accuracy of the given information. Whether the page offers "fact" or "opinion", it is still necessary to judge its appropriateness for your needs. Opinion can be accurate, but consumers of the information need to be aware that it is an opinion, not proven fact.

Example:
On the sample website of the National Soft Drink Association, the NSDA is disputing the claims of research published in *Lancet* (the British equivalent of the Journal of the American Medical Association) linking soft drinks to obesity in children. We recommend checking the credentials of *Lancet* to see who you should believe, a medical journal or a trade association.

Evaluating <u>Expert Opinion</u> in Web Resources

Questions to ask:
Are there reviews of the web site available?
Can you see a pattern in who links to the site?
What do the people linking to the site say about it?

Resources to use:

- Perform an <u>advanced search in Google</u>. By using the "page-specific search" function, you can see what other website link to the website your are reviewing. Other search engines offer similar search features.

- See if the pattern of sites linking to your site is of political perspectives, corporate ownership, and/or universities.
- Check the Scout Project, the Librarians' Index to the Internet, or ICYouSee: A Guide to the World Wide Web for reviews of your site.

So What?

You don't have to reinvent the wheel when it comes to evaluating information. Use the work others have done before you. If you can't find a review, it doesn't automatically mean your site is bad or useless. Reviews are just another clue to the appropriateness of the information.

http://www.augustana.edu/library/Services/webeval/index.htm

Evaluating Authority in Web Resources

Questions to ask:

Does the site have a section about its purpose?
Is the site offered as a public service, an advertisement, education, or opinion?
If advertising is present is it clearly labeled as such?
Whose site is this?
Who is sponsoring the creation and maintenance of the page?
Is the purpose of the sponsoring organization appropriate for your information needs?
Is there contact information to reach the author or sponsor for more information?
Who developed and wrote the material?
What is their perspective?
Can you verify his/her qualifications?

Resources to use:

Look for a link on the page to "about this organization" information. It could tell you everything you want to know. You just have to decide if they're painting an accurate picture!
Look for information on the sponsor outside of the web. Use *Encyclopedia of Associations* [REF AS 22 .E5], or go to the Lexis/Nexis Academic Universe database.
To assess the author's credibility, use Dissertation Abstracts Online, Lexis/Nexis Academic Universe, *Who's Who* [REF CT 120 .W5], or *Biography and Geneology Master Index* [REF CT 213 .B56].

So what?

Anyone with an internet connection and some software can set up a web page. There are clues that can help you recognize appropriate information. A writer could have a PhD in biology, but put up a web page about local politics. His academic credentials do not translate to being an authority on government. So you could rely on his information about genetics, but perhaps not on his information about political events.
When you use *Dissertation Abstracts* you may be able to find where and when a person wrote their disseration, and what their dissertation is about. The biographical information to be found in Lexis/Nexis, and *Who's Who* can help you learn about what a people have done in their career.
No one is totally objective. That doesn't mean their information is useless to you. It is important to recognize a bias, in order to know you need to research the other sides to an issue.

Example:

Work back up the hierarchy of directories that your webpage is located within to find out who is hosting the page, eg. http://www.augustana.edu/Users/Rewilliams/index.htm backs up to http://www.augustana.edu. You'll notice that there is a disclaimer at the end of the original web site   stating that "The views and opinions expressed in this page are strictly those of the page author. The contents have not been reviewed or approved by Augustana College." An individual's web site is not necessarily approved by the hosting institution.

The extension has clues about the origin of the site:

- .edu as an extension means an educational institution
- .com means a business
- .mil is a military site
- .gov is a government agency
- .net is a network
- .org is a non-profit organization

Evaluating <u>Coverage</u> in Web Resources

Questions to ask:

How old is the information the page is based upon?

Is the information provided relevant to your information need?

What are the dates covered by the site?

If there is a print edition of the work, do the different formats offer the same content?

What are the content limitations of the site?

Does it cover a specific aspect of a topic? A specific geographic area? Only men or only women?

Is there an indication that the page is completed and not "under construction"?

Resources to use:

- Look on the page itself for copyright and/or last updated dates. The site will provide (hopefully) most of the answers to the questions above.
- Check <u>ALiCat</u> to see if our library has a book on the same topic.

So What?

Just as when you use a book, you need appropriate information from your resource. You wouldn't use a kindergarten book in your Biology 101 bibliography, and you shouldn't use a fan web site for a critical review of a work of literature.

Example:

The *Catholic Encyclopedia* is available online and in print. The *New Catholic Encyclopedia* [Ref BX 841 .N44] ranges in copyright dates from 1967 to 1989. The online <u>*Catholic Encyclopedia*</u> has a copyright date of 2004, but the material is from the 1908 and 1913 editions.

Thomas Tredway Library ▪**Augustana College** ▪**639 38th Street, Rock Island, IL 61201**

MWSU Library Home » LibGuides Home » Evaluating Internet Sources   Admin Sign In

Evaluating Internet Sources   Tags: evaluation internet www web websites wikipedia
evaluation, internet, www, web, websites, wikipedia
Last update: May 13th, 2009 | URL: http://libguides.missouriwestern.edu/ie | Print/Mobile Guide | RSS Updates | SHARE

Why evaluate?   Evaluation Criteria   Wikipedia   Practice

Criteria for Evaluating Internet sites

Relevance- Is the page actually about your topic?
- Search engines don't look for context only occurrence

Accuracy- Is the information contained in the page accurate?
- Or is it wrong? Or blatantly false? Or one sided to influence you? Or an opinion presented as fact?
- Can you verify questionable information from another reliable source?

Author- Is there a way to determine the author's credentails?
- What is the author's educational background?
- Do they have a title, Dr, Ph.D, Ed.D?
- Has the author published other materials on this subject?
- Is an author even listed?
- If an organization is it one you can trust?
  - Do you know what they seek to accomplish?

Scholarship- Is the quality of information scholarly?
- Does the page include a list of references which the author consulted?
- Does the document include evidence to supports its arguments and the conclusion?
- Does the author possess the necessary knowledge and expertise to have written a quality piece?
- Does the site offer discredited theories and research to argue its point?
- Are there numerous spelling and grammatical errors?

Originality- Is the information presented new or just rehash of other peoples writings or links to to other pages?
- If not original are other authors given proper credit for their ideas?
- Can you verify that other's ideas are properly presented?

Bias-Is there bias apparent in the information? If yes, this not necessarily a bad thing as long as you aware of the bias.
- Is the page trying to sell you something?
- Who is the author and are they trying to persuade you?
- If the web page is published by an organization be aware they are presenting their point of view. For example,

- o The National Rifle Association(NRA) is trying to persuade you gun control is wrong.
- o The Coalition to Stop Gun Violence is trying to persuade you that gun control is right.

Currency- Is the information presented old or current?
- Does the page list a date of
  - o creation?
  - o updates?
  - o Is it updated frequently?
- Is the information presented current?
  - o This is especially important in science and technology.
- If links to other sites are provided is it current or outdated information?

Audience- Who is the target audience of the site?
- Grade school students?
- College students?
- Technical?
- Parents?
- Academics?

Web address- The address of a page can tell you about the sponsoring entity or the author of the page.
- .com is usually a profit entity
  - o This can be good if its CNN or the New York Times or the Kansas City Star
  - o This can be bad if its someone trying to sell you something or persuade you like Philip MorrisUsa.com
- .org is usually a non-profit organization or a lobbying group
  - o This can be good as many non-profuts conduct valauble research such the the American Heart Association
  - o This can be bad as many non-profits seek to offer only one side of an issue such as the National Rifle Association or the Brady Campaign to Prevent Gun Violence
- .edu is usually a four educational institution of higher learning
  - o This can be good as colleges and universities are leading producers of research
  - o This can be bad as it can lead to sites constructed, written and maitained by students with a lack of knowledge on the your topic

Links- Do links on the page work?
- Do links take you to "Not found" pages?
- Out of date or irrelevevant pages?
- Are you sent to advertisements?

Evaluating Web Resources

WEB SITES: Make sure to evaluate!!!

Use the **5W's** method: Who, What, When, Where, Why?

Who? Authority
- Who wrote the pages and are they an expert? Enter the author's name into a search engine to conduct a quick background check.
- Are there any links to in-depth information about the author or organization?
- Can you contact the company or author through a real world postal address or phone number? Can you confirm that the company or author is a credible, authoritative source of information?
- To check who owns the domain name, go to: http://www.networksolutions.com/whois/index.jsp
- To see what pages link to the site, type into **Google: link: nameofsite**

What? Objectivity – Goals of the Authors
- What is the purpose of the site? To sell? To inform? To persuade?
- Who is the intended audience?
- Does the site rely on loaded language or broad, unsubstantiated statements?
- Is emotion used as a means of persuasion?
- Does the site offer more than one viewpoint?
- Does the Web site offer links of further in-depth resources??

When? Currenc*y*
- When was the site created?
- When was the site last updated?
- Do the links work?
- What's the copyright status of material found on the site?

Where? Accuracy – Reliability
- Where does the information come from?
- Learn to deconstruct a Uniform Resource Locator (better known as a URL or "site address"). Using this URL from the *Assumption College Library* as an example:

http://www.assumption.edu/dept/Library/libraryindex.html
http://www – The "http" notation here indicates that this is a hypertext document (most online documents are in this format). The "www" is short form for the "World Wide Web," where all Web sites reside

assumption.edu/ – the second part of a URL contains the domain name of the person or organization hosting the Web site — in this case, Assumption. The ".edu" which follows indicates that the site is hosted by an educational institution.

dept/Library/libraryindex.html- The last section maps out the pathway of directories and sub directories leading to the page you are on. For this particular page on the Assumption Library site, "dept/" indicates that you are in a specific department, in this case, the library. The final URL entry (in this case "library index") indicates the name of the page or document you have arrived at. "Html" indicates the code or format that it has been created in.

~ Sometimes you might see a "user" reference or tilde (~) symbol in a sub directory, followed by a name. This indicates that you may be on a personal Web page that is being hosted by an ISP (Internet Service Provider).

- Where can I look to find out more about the producer/sponsor?

The type of organization behind a Web site can give some clues to its credibility.

.gov	In the US, .gov applies to federal departments. In Canada, provincial governments use .gov followed by a provincial abbreviation and .ca
.us	Schools, educational organizations, libraries, museums and some government departments may be registered under a 2-digit country of origin code, such as .ca, .us or .au
.edu	The United States originally created .edu to indicate American colleges and universities offering 4-year degree programs. Most Canadian universities tend to use .ca.
.org **.com** **.net**	Back in the early days of the Web: **.org** indicated a wide assortment of groups, including non-profit organizations; **.com** indicated commercial organizations; and **.net** was intended for organizations directly involved in Internet operations, such as Internet service providers**Now, anyone can apply for, and use, these letters in their domain names!** For example, the Web site for the YWCA in Calgary, ends with .com, in Vancouver, it ends with .org, and in Montreal, .ca!

Why? Coverage – value of the content- Is the internet even the best place to go?
- Why is this information useful for my purpose?
- Why should I use this information?
- Why is this page better than another?
- Can I get the information faster off-line?
- Does the online material I'm finding suit my needs?
- Am I able to verify this information?

Assumption College 2008, as adapted from Kathy Schrock's "5 W's of Website Evaluation (1998)," and Media Awareness Network's, "5 W's of Cyberspace (2008)." Revised 10/27/09, d'Alzon Library.

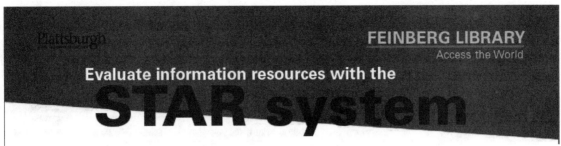

Scholarship, Timeliness, Authority, Relevance

Scholarship: Evidence of careful investigation of fact and analysis of opinion.
Questions to ask: Is the information accurate when checked against other sources? Is the writing style popular, technical, or academic in tone and language? Is this new information or a summarization of older information? How reliable and error-free is the information? Is there evidence of potential bias? Does the author have a specifi c agenda or point-of-view? Does the author explain where the information was obtained? Does the information include a bibliography or list of sources used?

Timeliness: Currency of the publication and of its bibliography. *Questions to ask:* Is the publication date clearly stated? When was the book last published or the web page page last revised? Is it maintained and updated regularly? Are any links on the web page up-to-date and useable? Is the information current or historical enough for your topic? How do the publication dates in the bibliography or list of sources compare to the publication date of the information resource?

Authority: Expertise, knowledge and experience. *Questions to ask:* Is it clear who is authoring, sponsoring or publishing the information? Is the sponsor or publisher legitimate? Is it clear who wrote the information? Are the qualifi cations (educational degrees, job experience, eyewitness status) of the author clearly stated? How does the author know about this topic? Is the author affi liated with an institution or organization? Is that institution connected to the topic? Is there contact information available for the author of the document?

Relevance: Direct focus on the topic or research question. *Questions to ask:* Does the information cover the subject adequately? Are there inexplicable omissions? What is the purpose of the information,i.e., to inform, convince, or sell? What does it contribute to the literature in the fi eld? Who is the intended audience based on content, tone, and style? What is the overall value of the content compared to the range of resources on the topic?

Randolph-Macon College

Evaluating Sources

Not all information is good, valid information. Evaluation means that you look carefully at your information sources to determine whether the source is reliable and appropriate for your information need. You should always evaluate any information source you use.

Key Criteria
Other Considerations
Evaluation and the Internet

Key Criteria

There are seven key criteria to consider when evaluating your sources:

Authority: the credentials of the author(s) and to the publisher of the information.
Who wrote or compiled the information? Who published it and why?

Currency: date of publication and the time period covered by the information.
Is the publication current or historic? Does it matter?

Accuracy: the overall reliability and correctness of the information.
Are the facts and statistics correct and verifiable?

Scope: the completeness of the coverage.
Is the publication comprehensive or selective? What is the focus of the source? Is it relevant to your information need?

Objectivity: the point of view taken in the material.
Is there an obvious bias or does it appear to be relatively objective? Is the author simply providing factual information or expressing an opinion?

Documentation: whether the material cites the sources of the information that is presented.
Do the authors or editors include references or is the information compiled from unknown sources?

Presentation: how the material is organized and supplemented.
Are there good access points such as a table of contents or an index? Are there visual aids to enhance or explain the information?

Other Considerations
Is the source popular or scholarly? Which will better fulfill your information need?
Is the source primary or secondary? Which will better fulfill your information need?

Evaluation and the Internet

Evaluating sources online is very similar to evaluating print sources. In addition to the key criteria and other considerations, look at the domain of the website.

The **domain** is the main part of the address; for example, the domain of Randolph-Macon College is www.rmc.edu. The last three letters, or domain suffix, will help you determine the authority and objectivity of a website.

These are some of the most common domain suffixes:

.com Commercial site, available to anyone.
HostSite

.edu Educational institutions, regulated by Educause and the U.S. Department of Commerce.
Randolph-Macon College

.gov Federal government site.
Library of Congress

.info Informative site, available to anyone.
Libraries in the United States

.int Site of an international organization, regulated by the Internet Assigned Numbers Authority.
World Health Organization

.mil Military site, regulated by the U.S. Department of Defense.
United States Air Force

.net Network or commercial site, available to anyone.
Academic Info

.org Organizational site, available to anyone.
American Heart Association

Countries also have their own 2-letter codes, such as .au for Australia.

For additional information about evaluating Internet sources, see Critical Evaluation of Resources on the Internet (University of Alberta Libraries).

McGraw-Page Library, P. O. Box 5005; 305 Henry Street, Ashland VA, 23005-5505

Evaluating Web Site Addresses

One quick way of evaluating web sites is to look at the web site address or URL at the top of your web browser. Web site addresses (also called domain names) can tell you where the web site is coming from.

.com = A commercial web site. The quality of commercial web sites can vary. You might find information from a well-known national news publication like Time (http://www.time.com/time/) or the New York Times (http://www.nytimes.com/). You might find a digital library (http://www.bartleby.com/) You could also find web sites that are just trying to sell you something.

.org = A non-profit organization. You could find information from a professional scientific organization (http://www.apa.org), an international organization (http://www.imf.org/), or an advocacy organization (http://www.peta.org). You can find good information on .org sites, but do some fact checking -- are you finding similar information in journal articles or books? Does the organization seem to have a particular slant or bias, and are they only presenting one point of view? Just because a site has a .org domain name, it doesn't mean that their motives aren't suspect. For example, the web site www.martinlutherking.org is run by a white supremacist organization.

.net = Network organization. The web site may be part of a internet hosting company, or it could be a commercial or non-profit site.

.gov = Government web site. Government web sites can be a rich and varied source of information, ranging from the US Government's web portal (http://firstgov.gov), to sites for specific government agencies, (http://www.census.gov), to a digital collection like the Library of Congress's American Memory project (http://memory.loc.gov/).

.mil = Reserved for military organizations like the army (http://www.army.mil/).

.edu = Educational institutions. Web sites of colleges and universities will have .edu web sites as well as web sites from high schools or elementary schools. You might find an online journal (http://www.journals.uchicago.edu/ApJ/) or a page maintained by a department of Asian Studies (http://asnic.utexas.edu/asnic.html), or a professor's personal web site like the Periodic Table of Comic Books (http://www.uky.edu/Projects/Chemcomics/).

International Web sites also have identifiable domain names. Usually the name of the country will be a two letter abbreviation (.ca is for Canada, .de is for Germany. A list of country abbreviations is available at: (http://www.norid.no/domenenavnbaser/domreg-alpha.html).

.Com domain names become **.co** on non-US sites. So, the web site address (http://www.bbc.co.uk/) indicates that it is a commercial site from the United Kingdom.

Widener University

Reach higher. Go farther. Choose Widener.

Quick Clicks | SEARCH | GO >

About Widener | Admissions | Academics | News & Events | Campus Life | Athletics | Alumni | Civic Mission

How to Recognize an Advocacy Web Page

An Advocacy Web Page is one sponsored by an organization attempting to influence public opinion (that is, one trying to sell ideas). The URL address of the page frequently ends in **.org** (organization).

Examples:

- National Abortion and Reproductive Rights Action League
- The National Right to Life Committee
- The Democratic Party
- The Republican Party

How to Recognize a Business/Marketing Web Page

A Business/Marketing Web Page is one sponsored by a commercial enterprise (usually it is a page trying to promote or sell products). The URL address of the page frequently ends in **.com** (commercial).

Examples:

- Adobe Systems, Inc.
- The Coca Cola Company

How to Recognize a News Web Page

A News Web Page is one whose primary purpose is to provide extremely current information. The URL address of the page usually ends in **.com** (commercial).

Examples:

- *The Philadelphia Inquirer*
- *USA Today*
- *CNN*

How to Recognize a Personal Web Page

A Personal Web Page is one published by an individual who may or may not be affiliated with a larger institution. Although the URL address of the page may have a variety of endings (e.g. .com, .edu, etc.), a tilde (~) is frequently embedded somewhere in the URL.

How to Recognize an Informational Web Page

An Informational Web Page is one whose purpose is to present factual information. The URL Address frequently ends in **.edu** or **.gov**, as many of these pages are sponsored by educational institutions or government agencies.

Examples:

- Dictionaries
- Thesauri
- Directories
- Statistical Data

Questions to Ask About the Web Page

Note: The greater number of questions listed below answered "**yes**", the more likely it is you can determine whether the source is of high information quality.

Criterion #1: AUTHORITY Is it clear who is responsible for the contents of the page?

1. Is there a link to a page describing the purpose of the sponsoring organization?
2. Is there a way of verifying the legitimacy of the page's sponsor? That is, is there a phone number or postal address to contact for more information? (Simply an email address is not enough.)
3. Is it clear who wrote the material and are the author's qualifications for writing on this topic clearly stated?
4. If the material is protected by copyright, is the name of the copyright holder given?

Criterion #2: ACCURACY

1. 1. Are the sources for any factual information clearly listed so they can be verified in another source?
2. Is the information free of grammatical, spelling, and typographical errors? (These kinds of errors not only indicate a lack of quality control, but can actually produce inaccuracies in information.)
3. Is it clear who has the ultimate responsibility for the accuracy of the content of the material?
4. If there are charts and/or graphs containing statistical data, are the charts and/or graphs clearly labeled and easy to read?

Criterion #3: OBJECTIVITY

1. Is the information provided as a public service?
2. Is the information free of advertising?
3. If there is any advertising on the page, is it clearly differentiated from the informational content?

Criterion #4: CURRENCY

1. 1. Are there dates on the page to indicate:
   o When the page was written?
   o When the page was first placed on the Web?
   o When the page was last revised?
2. Are there any other indications that the material is kept current?
3. If material is presented in graphs and/or charts, is it clearly stated when the data was gathered?
4. If the information is published in different editions, is it clearly labeled what edition the page is from?

Criterion #5: COVERAGE

1. Is there an indication that the page has been completed, and is not still under construction?
2. If there is a print equivalent to the Web page, is there a clear indication of whether the entire work is available on the Web or only parts of it?
3. If the material is from a work which is out of copyright (as is often the case with a dictionary or thesaurus) has there been an effort to update the material to make it more current?

How do you evaluate resources?

For many academic research projects, instructors will require that you research many different types of resources. Often it is difficult to recognize the value of a particular resource. Below is a list of six criteria for evaluating resources, and questions or topics that you should consider when identifying the best and most appropriate books, articles, and web sites for your research.

Remember that, unlike books and articles which are approved by publishers, web sites can be created by anyone and made available on the World Wide Web freely. That means that even children create web sites on many topics, so you need to consider the following criteria and questions carefully.

Criteria	Books	Articles	Web Sites
ACCURACY -- Are sources of information and factual data listed, and available for cross-checking?	--Is there a table of contents? --Does it include footnotes and a bibliography?	--Does it include footnotes and a bibliography?	--Does it include footnotes and a bibliography?
AUTHORITY --Who is responsible for the work and what are their qualifications and associations, and can you verify them?	--Does it identify the author? Is there biographical information or do you need to look elsewhere? Is the author an expert in the field? Is s/he associated with an organization that does research on this topic? --Who is the publisher? Is it a university press, a commercial publisher, a professional or trade association, the government, or is it self-published?	--Does it identify the author? Is there biographical information or do you need to look elsewhere? Is the author an expert in the field? Is s/he associated with an organization that does research on this topic? --In what type of journal/magazine does the article appear? Is it a scholarly journal, trade journal, or a magazine?	--Does it identify the author? Is there biographical information or do you need to look elsewhere? Is the author an expert in the field? Is s/he associated with an organization that does research on this topic? What does the domain name tell you about the location of the web site **.edu** = educational institutions **.com** = commercial/ business organizations **.org** = non-profit/ other organizations **.gov** = government agencies **.net** = network resources
OBJECTIVITY --Are biases clearly stated? Are any political/ ideological agenda hidden to disguise its purpose? Do they use a misleading name or	--Who is the intended audience? Is the book for general readers? Students? Researchers? --Why was the book written? To inform? persuade? teach? entertain? --Is there a preface or	--Who is the intended audience? Is the article in a publication that is written for general readers? students? researchers? --Why was the article written? To inform? persuade? teach?	--Who is the intended audience? Is the web site written for children? general readers? researchers? --Why was the web site created? To inform? persuade? teach? entertain? just for fun? --What are the affiliations of

other means to do this?	introduction to identify objectives?	entertain? --What are the affiliations of the author?	the author?
CURRENCY --How up-to-date is the information?	--What is the copyright date (located on the title page)? --Is the information up-to-date, out-of-date, or does the information never go out-of-date? --How current are the sources listed in the bibliography (dates)?	--What is the date of the article? --How current are the sources listed in the bibliography (dates)?	--Are the dates listed? --When was the web site first created? --When was the last time that the web site was revised? --Are the links still viable? Do any linked sites identified still exist?
COVERAGE --What is the focus of the work?	--Is there a table of contents? an index? --Is the book organized logically and/or in a manner which makes it easy to understand? --Are there appendices to supplement the main text?	--What are the affiliations of the author? --Is there an abstract? --Does the article cover the topic comprehensively, partially, or is it an overview? <u>Is it primary, secondary, or tertiary information?</u>	--Are there clear headings to indicate an outline to determine what aspects of the topic are covered? --Is there a Table of Contents? an Index? an Abstract? --Is navigation within the web site clear? --Does the article cover the topic comprehensively, partially, or is it an overview? <u>Is it primary, secondary, or tertiary information?</u>
RELEVANCY --Does the resource actually cover the topic you are researching?	--Does the book support or refute an argument? --Does the book give examples? survey results? research findings? case studies? --Is it really research? or just commentary?	--Does the article support or refute an argument? --Does the article give examples? survey results? research findings? case studies? --Is it really research? or just commentary?	--Does the web site support or refute an argument? --Does the web site give examples? survey results? research findings? case studies? link to other useful and recommended sites? --Is it really research? or just commentary? --Does it cover the topic as well as other types of sources (books, articles, etc.)?

**Tarleton State University
Libraries**

Unit 8

EVALUATING INTERNET RESOURCES

Internet resources are vast, but often are not reviewed thoroughly. As a result, many contain unreliable information. Before using Internet resources, evaluate them using criteria like those listed below, which are grouped in six categories.

Each category offers a series of evaluative questions and gives suggested ways to find answers to the questions. Links to more criteria are provided after the last category.

PURPOSE & AUDIENCE

• What is the resource's purpose? Is the purpose stated or implied?
• Does the resource try to persuade, inform, or sell something? How so?
• Is the site a primary or secondary source?
• Who is its intended audience? How might this influence its content?
• Is advertising included (pop-up ads, banners, inserts, etc.)? Might it impact the content or indicate the resource's purpose?

Checking purpose and audience:
-- Read the purpose/mission statement for the resource, if available.
-- Check the home page for the resource.
-- Read the article submission guidelines, if present.
-- Notice the tone and terminology used in the resource.
-- Note the presence/absence and types of advertising and announcements.
-- Examine the types of information, evidence, and examples used.
-- Search the Internet for reviews of the resource.
-- Check the domain: non-profit organization (org), commercial site (com), US higher education site (edu), and so on.

AUTHORITY

• Who is the author or sponsor of the web resource?
• Does the author have adequate qualifications/expertise?
• Where is the resource located (i.e. in a larger site, an e-journal, and so on)?
• Is the work cited in other works or linked to by other sites?
• Are the author's qualifications given? Where is the author employed?
• Who is the sponsoring agency, organization, or institution for the resource?
• What are the agency's/organization's credentials and reputation?
• Has the author or agency/organization created other web resources?
• What domain is shown in the URL. For example, *gov* in *whitehouse.gov* indicates a federal government domain.

Checking the author's authority:
-- Use biographical dictionaries and critical essays to investigate the author.
-- Search appropriate databases & the Internet for citations to the resource.
-- Read articles that cite/critique the resource (and other works by the author).
-- Find out if the author has written other articles, reports, etc. on the topic.
-- Check the online home page for the resource or its sponsoring organization.
-- **WhoIs web site** can help you identify the sponsor of a site.

ACCURACY & RELIABILITY

• Is a bibliography or reference list available so information can be verified?
• Does the web resource offer trustworthy information?
• Is the information protected by copyright? Who is the copyright holder?
• Does the resource indicate editorial quality (free of errors)?
• Can the people/agencies listed as authors/sponsors be verified?
• Is contact information given? (email & physical addresses, phone)

Checking accuracy and reliability:
-- Examine the text for evidence of careful research.
-- Check if data, statistics, and facts are documented (and current).
-- Double-check information in the resource with other sources.
-- Read critiques and analyses in reputable sources.
-- Determine if the resource is peer-reviewed, editor-reviewed, etc.
-- Examine the quality of items listed in the bibliography, if one is present.
-- Check the sponsor/site type: academic, commercial, personal, etc.

OBJECTIVITY

- Is the information biased or balanced, subjective or objective?
- Is the text mostly fact or opinion? Is that appropriate?
- Does the text acknowledge the above?
- Does the author use logical or emotional appeal?

Checking objectivity:
-- Examine the writer's claims. Are they logical and reasonable?
-- Examine the evidence presented. Is it adequate and credible?
-- Read critical essays about and responses to the resource.
-- Notice the presence/absence and types of advertising.

CURRENCY

- Was the web resource previously published elsewhere?
- When was the web resource first produced? Is that important?
- When was it put online? Is that important?
- When was it last updated? Is that important?
- Is the information current? Should it be?
- Are current research findings and/or theories evident? Should they be?
- Do links work? Do they lead to quality resources? Are they up-to-date?

Checking work's currency:
-- Check dates on references, if any are given.
-- Check dates given for any data presented in the text.
-- Compare the information with that presented in other sources.
-- Check the publishing history (date on the resource, notes about previous publishing, links on other sites, update information, etc.).

COVERAGE

- Does the web resource adequately cover its topic?
- Does it claim to present results of research and/or scholarly projects?
- Can claims of scholarship be confirmed?
- Does it include information from various resource types (print & online)?
- Does the resource present original ideas or rehash those of others?
- Are significant aspects of the topic omitted?
- Are omissions acknowledged and explained?

• Do links go to other pages in the same site, to other sites, or both?
• Do research results and documentation style adhere to practices normally used in that discipline?

Checking coverage:
-- Examine the introductory paragraphs and editor's notes about the article.
-- Analyze the breadth of content. Does it meet expectations?
-- Read articles/other resources that discuss/analyze the resource in question.
-- Compare the resource with similar works.
-- Follow links and evaluate linked resources.

Five Criteria for evaluating Web pages

The Criteria	How to interpret...
1. Accuracy of Web Documents • Who wrote the page and can you contact him or her? • What is the purpose of the document and why was it produced? • Is this person qualified to write this document?	**Accuracy** • Make sure author provides e-mail or a contact address/phone number. • Know the distinction between author and Webmaster.
2. Authority of Web Documents • Who published the document and is it separate from the "Webmaster?" • Check the domain of the document— what institution publishes this document?	**Authority** • What credentials are listed for the author(s)? • Where is the document published? Check URL domain.
3. Objectivity of Web Documents • What goals/objectives does this page meet? • How detailed is the information? • What opinions (if any) are expressed by the author? Are they supported with documented research?	**Objectivity** • Determine if page is a mask for advertising; if so information might be biased. • View any Web page as you would an infomercial on television. Ask yourself why was this written and for whom?
4. Currency of Web Documents • When was it produced? • When was it updated? • How up-to-date are the links (if any)?	**Currency** • How many dead links are on the page? • Are the links current or updated regularly? • Is the information on the page outdated?
5. Coverage of the Web Documents • Are the links (if any) evaluated and do they complement the documents theme? • Is it all images or a balance of text and images? • Is the information presented cited correctly?	**Coverage** • If page requires special software to view the information, how much are you missing if you don't have the software? • Is it free, or is there a fee, to obtain the information? • Is there an option for text only, or frames, or a suggested browser for better viewing?

Putting it all together...
- **Accuracy.** If the page lists the author and institution that published the page and provides a way of contacting him/her, and . . .
- **Authority.** If the page lists the author credentials and its domain is preferred (.edu, .gov, .org, or .net), and . . .
- **Objectivity.** If the page provides accurate information with limited advertising

and it is objective in presenting the information, and . . .

- **Currency.** If the page is current and updated regularly (as stated on the page) and the links (if any) are also up-to-date, and . . .
- **Coverage.** If information can be viewed properly--not limited to fees, browser technology, or software requirement, then . . .
- **Consider using the site as a resource, but only as supplemental research. The Web should never be your main or only source for a research project.**

And Don't Forget...

- **Technical Problems.** Web pages often disappear, change addresses, or simply go "down." If you are planning on using a site as a resource, be note the date you accessed the site in your citation.
- **Links.** Many web pages provide links to other, similar web sources. The quality of all these linked resources, however, may be vastly different. Use the same evaluation criteria on every page you encounter, even if it's link from a reputable source.
- **Context.** Search engines (like Yahoo, Alta Vista) often retrieve web pages out of context. Always try to return to the home page of any source you use.
- **Check out some web pages on evaluating web pages:**

  The Good, The Bad & The Ugly: or,
  Why It's a Good Idea to Evaluate Web Sources
  http://lib.nmsu.edu/instruction/eval.html

  Tips for Evaluating A World Wide Web Search
  http://web.uflib.ufl.edu/admin/wwwtips.pdf

Elon University, Carol Grotnes Belk Library, Elon, NC

LIBRARIES, MEDIA SERVICES, & ARCHIVES   ST. CATHERINE UNIVERSITY

Library Home   Hours   Contact Us   Search our Site

˅ Books, Articles & More   ˅ Help with Research   ˅ Library Services   ˅ About the Library

🔍 Search CLICnet: [＿＿＿＿＿] in: [Books and more ⬥] (Go)   [Quick Links... ⬥] (Go)

Evaluating Internet Sources

Learning how to evaluate good sources of information will help you long after you graduate from college. Learn more by checking out these other websites or by talking to a librarian (call 651-690-6652 for help).

Authorship
- Is the author clearly stated?
- What are the author's qualifications? Institutional affiliation?
- Is the author well-known and respected in his or her field?
- Is the author mentioned in a positive way by another authority you trust?
- If none of the above is present, is there contact information given (other than an email address) that would allow you to verify the author?

Example of:	*Source*	Why?
Poor authorship:	Electronic Frontier Foundation	This website is sponsored by an organization promoting free speech. This will not neessarily give you unbiased information.
Scholarly authorship:	Library of Congress: Links to Historical Documents	This is a website from the US government that includes the actual text of the First Amendment.

Publishing Body
- Is the name of any organization given on the page?
- Is this organization recognized in the field you are studying? Try to use information from government agencies, trade or professional associations, major universities, or research centers.
- Does the page actually reside in an individual's personal Internet account? This is frequently the case if the URL contains a tilde (~), (e.g. http://www.someschool.edu/~olson/get_rich.html or http://www.geocities.com/johnsmith/mywebpage.html). Approach this type of resource with caution.
- Check to see if the URL moves or disappears abruptly. Reliable Web sites establish markers to help you easily find new locations of pages.

Example of:	Source	Why?
Poor publishing body:	In Defense of Affirmative Action	This collection of articles is published online only. There is no contact information given and may have dubious origins. Proceed with caution!
Reputable publishing body:	Affirmative Action (Ohio University)	This website is from Ohio University, an actual brick and mortar institution. We can assume that it has good information, although we should still check other sources.

Point of View or Bias

- Is the author or publisher trying to promote a particular philosophical viewpoint or political agenda? Try to determine this by examining the URL and by reading other pages on the Web site. Businesses, political groups, and advocacy groups usually have some bias.
- Does the Web site have a stated purpose?
- Is the page an advertisement for something?
- Is this Web site hosted by or affiliated with an organization or Web server with a political or philosophical agenda?

Example of:	Source	Why?
Biased webpage:	Abortion TV: The Internet's #1 abortion information source	Despite claiming to be "#1 information source," this website is biased. Although biased webpages may have vaulable information, be sure to read the official opinions before using facts for research.
Unbiased webpage:	Medline Plus: Abortion	This website from the National Institutes of Health gives a medical definition of the controversial topic of abortion and does not express opinions.

Accuracy

- Did you find this document through a link on another page whose quality you trust?
- Does the document cite (or link to) other sources or include a bibliography?
- For a research document, is there an explanation of how the data was gathered and interpreted?
- Could you verify the background information that was used?
- Can the author be contacted by mail or e-mail for clarification or to be informed of new information?
- Is the text well-written? Is it free of grammatical, spelling, and other typographical errors?
- Is it clear who has the ultimate responsibility for the accuracy of the material?

Example of:	Source	Why?
Questionable accuracy:	Children and Television Violence	This website provides facts and figures without any references and quotations without citations. Such claims should be substantiated.
More accuracy:	Violence on Television	This website provides the credentials for the researchers in this area and also supplies a list of additional resources.

Currency

- Is it clear when the page was created? Copyrighted? Last updated?
- If the text is based on another source, does it indicate the date of that source (e.g., "Based on 1990 US Census data...")?

Example of:	Source	Why?
Older information:	The Truth About Stem Cells	While this website includes a date, the article on stem cells is from 2001. Three years can make a big difference in the world of science and other areas.
Current information:	Stem Cell Research Foundation	This website provides listings of articles by date so that you can be sure you're getting recent information on the topic.

Appropriateness

- Did you get the best information? Did you miss any good Web sites?
- Does a more "traditional" source in the library, such as a reference book or journal article database, provide superior information?
- If you found this website through an Internet search engine such as Google, you need to know how this search engine decides the placements of results. Some engines allow companies to pay for top placement.

Example of:	Source	Why?
Web information:	National Atlas	Although the US government can supply us with wonderful maps, they're easier to view in book form.
Print information:	*MacMillian Color Atlas of the States* G1200 .M4 1996	This Atlas is located in the Reference Room in the Library. Sometimes it is easier and more useful to consult print formats such as books.

Eckerd College | Library Tutorial

Web Sites   Lesson 1

Many of you use Google and Wikipedia as your main information sources. Now that you're in college (woo-hoo!), you will use more reliable, scholarly sources such as books and database articles.

There is a place for websites in your quest for information-government documents, research reports, statistical data, and newspaper articles for instance, but now that you have access to more advanced sources, you won't need to use the web as much.

NEXT►

Web Sites   Lesson 2

It is important to evaluate a website before you decide to use it as an information source. There are five factors to consider for evaluation:

Authorship
Purpose/Audience
Bias
Date
URL

Lets take a closer look...

 ◄BACK   NEXT►

Web Sites   Lesson 3

Let's take a closer look:

Google search for Martin Luther King Jr.

One of the first sites in the list is The Martin Luther King, Jr., Research and Education Institute. When we visit this site, we want to check for authorship.

Always look for a link "About Us" or "About the Author" to determine who is responsible for the content on the site.

The Institute is a research center at Stanford University and the description indicates all materials are of a professional and scholarly nature.

Let's go back to the Google results and scroll further down the page.

This one might be also be helpful: Martin Luther King Jr. - A True Historical Examination. There is no link for information about the author, but upon closer inspection, we see a "Hosted" link at the bottom that points to a White Pride organization. What do you suppose their "true historical examination" will be?

Remember, just because Bob's Fabulous Web Page of Dolphins is well designed and has information, it's useless if Bob is some guy who dropped out of high school, lives in his parent's basement, and works at the mall.

 BACK   NEXT

Web Sites   Lesson 3 Demo

Martin Luther King Jr. - Google Search - Mozilla Firefox

File Edit View History Bookmarks Tools Help

http://www.google.com/search?hl=en&q=Martin+Luther+King+Jr.&   Google

Web Images Video News Maps Gmail more ▼   cpaquet@gmail.com | My Account | Sign out

Google | Martin Luther King Jr. | Search   Advanced Search
Preferences

New! View and manage your web history

Web Books News Images   Results **1 - 10** of about **5,090,000** for Martin Luther King Jr.. (0.12 seconds)

Book results for **Martin Luther King Jr.**

Why We Can't Wait - by **Martin Luther King**, ... - 176 pages
I Have a Dream - by **Jr Martin Luther King**, James Melvin Washington - 256 pages
The Autobiography of **Martin Luther King, Jr.** - by Clayborne--Ed. "Carson, ... - 416 pages

Martin Luther King, Jr. - Wikipedia, the free encyclopedia
Martin Luther King, Jr., (January 15, 1929 – April 4, 1968) was one of the main leaders of the American civil rights movement, a political activist, ...

Sponsored Links

Martin Luther King, Jr.
Let's honor his vision for freedom, opportunity & justice for all.
www.BuildTheDream.org

Martin Luther King, Jr.
The **King** Research and Education

Web Sites Lesson 4

Purpose and Audience is the second area of evaluation. You always want to ask yourself why a webpage exists- Is someone trying to sell me something? Is someone presenting a personal opinion? Is someone publishing credible research? And for whom was this information intended?

Let's search for global warming

One of the first sites is the US EPA Global Warming site

The Environmental Protection Agency is a large government organization that disseminates and analyzes scientific data on the environment. When we click on Past Climate Change, there are links to data within the document and a list of References at the bottom.

Government agencies combined with documents sources and citations are signs of credibility.

Let's go back to our Google search and take a closer look at another site: Global warming, photography, pictures, photos, climate change.

Here, the purpose of the site is to sell us a book of nature photography (note the author link at the bottom takes us to the author's photography website). Books with pretty pictures are fine, but do you think this would be a useful site for data on global warming?

Don't assume that just because it's on the web, it's a useful research resource. Always remember Bob who lives in his parent's basement.

◀ BACK   NEXT ▶

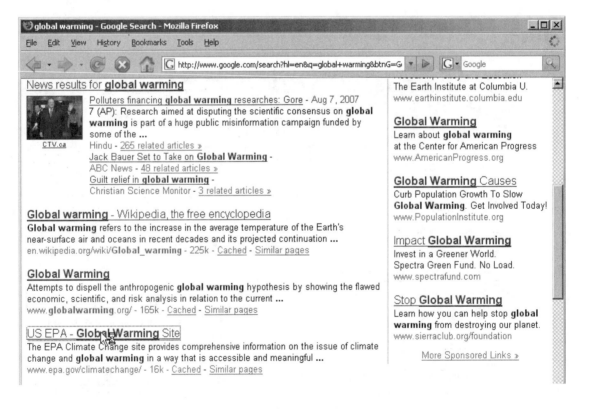

Web Sites Lesson 5

Bias is the third area of evaluation.

The web is the best (if not only) place to publish extreme and outrageous viewpoints and opinions. Obvious bias is easy to spot, but sometimes political, religious, or social bias can be more subtle.

When we do search for gun control, the first site, GunCite, contains links to essays and statistics. Upon further investigation, we see that the language is not professional or scholarly and there is a clear political message against gun control.

Let's look at another site in the Google results list: Brady Campaign to Prevent Gun Violence. Here we see strong language in favor of gun control and although the site has a professional appearance, the language is not scholarly or objective.

Again, Bob might have some opinions that he can't publish or make available anywhere else but on the web.

Always be skeptical! Web content hasn't necessarily been through a review process like newspaper, magazine, and journal articles have.

 ◀BACK   NEXT▶

Here's another website on tobacco use:

http://www.who.int/tobacco/en/

The author of this website is:

- ○ A college student working on a class project
- ○ A guy named Bob who lives in his parent's basement
- ○ The World Health Organization, Geneva Switzerland
- ○ A newsletter publisher reporting on health issues

There is an "About WHO" link clearly visible at the top of the page defining the mission and history of the World Health Organization. Since they are the health authority within the United Nations, the content is appropriate for research use.

The purpose of this website is to:

- ○ Sell me books and articles for my research
- ○ Distribute reports, news, and statistics on world health issues
- ○ Sign members up for a health action electronic newsletter
- ○ Send copies of birth certificates to colleges and universities

The group is a respected international organization which regularly conducts research and observes global health trends. Their purpose is to disseminate information to governments, health agencies, and researchers (such as yourself!).

How to Evaluate Information on the Web | Online Tutorial

After listening to the <u>online tutorial</u>, answer the following questions.

1. Give two characteristics of the *OncoLink* site that help make it clear whether this is a reliable place to go for cancer information.

_____

_____

2. What kind of research might the *Smoker's With Attitude* Website be useful for?

_____

_____

3. List two pieces of information that, if added to the *Sports and the Arts Without Tobacco* page from the World Health Organization, would help make it a more useful source for your research.

_____

_____

4. Explain under what circumstances the *martinlutherking.org* site might be useful for research.

_____

_____

5. List two characteristics of *the kingcenter.org* site that make it a more objective tool for research than the *martinlutherking.org* site.

_____

_____

(Portions of tutorial following)

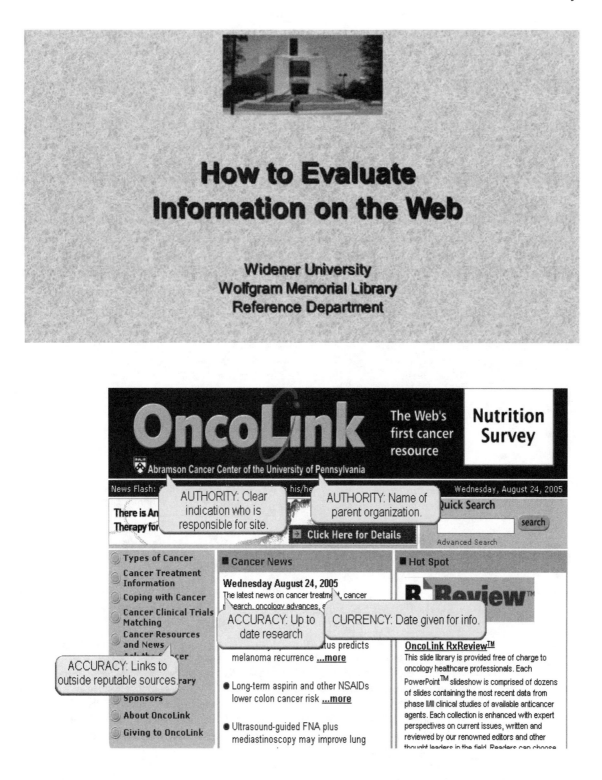

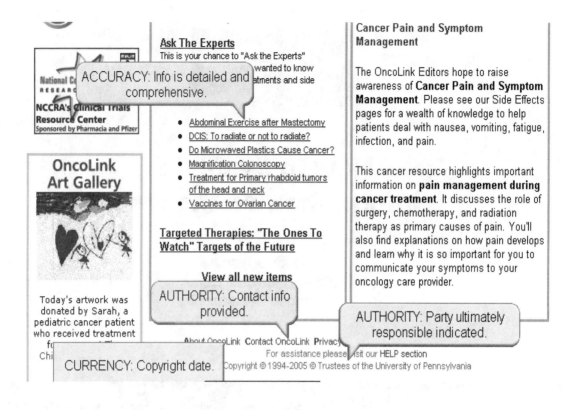

Ask The Experts

This is your chance to "Ask the Experts" ... wanted to know ...tments and side

ACCURACY: Info is detailed and comprehensive.

- Abdominal Exercise after Mastectomy
- DCIS: To radiate or not to radiate?
- Do Microwaved Plastics Cause Cancer?
- Magnification Colonoscopy
- Treatment for Primary rhabdoid tumors of the head and neck
- Vaccines for Ovarian Cancer

Targeted Therapies: "The Ones To Watch" Targets of the Future

View all new items

AUTHORITY: Contact info provided.

About OncoLink Contact OncoLink Privacy
For assistance please visit our HELP section
Copyright © 1994-2005 © Trustees of the University of Pennsylvania

CURRENCY: Copyright date.

OncoLink Art Gallery

Today's artwork was donated by Sarah, a pediatric cancer patient who received treatment fo...

Cancer Pain and Symptom Management

The OncoLink Editors hope to raise awareness of **Cancer Pain and Symptom Management**. Please see our Side Effects pages for a wealth of knowledge to help patients deal with nausea, vomiting, fatigue, infection, and pain.

This cancer resource highlights important information on **pain management during cancer treatment**. It discusses the role of surgery, chemotherapy, and radiation therapy as primary causes of pain. You'll also find explanations on how pain develops and learn why it is so important for you to communicate your symptoms to your oncology care provider.

AUTHORITY: Party ultimately responsible indicated.

NCCRA's Clinical Trials Resource Center — Sponsored by Pharmacia and Pfizer

---

AUTHORITY: No indication of who is responsible for page or site.

SPORTS AND THE ARTS WITHOUT TOBACCO

Play it tobacco free!

SOME EXAMPLES OF SPONSORSHIP OF SPORT AND ARTS BY TOBACCO COMPANIES

AUTHORITY: No authors listed.

As an increasing number of countries are banning various forms of direct advertis... companies have been shifting their attention to indirect promotion of their products by such means as sponsorship of sports and arts events. For a relatively minor donation to culture, tobacco companies buy their way into the advertising market, where they spend millions of dollars ensuring that the public remains familiar with the colours, logos and images of their brands. Studies confirm that the small fraction of money that may be received from tobacco companies for sponsorship of the sports and arts contrasts strongly with the societal costs that result from

ACCURACY: No sources listed for presented information.

In many cases, sponsorship also allows tobacco companies to reach a global audience, and is a imaginative way to circumvent advertising bans of tobacco products on television. Sponsorship is believed to be an effective way of

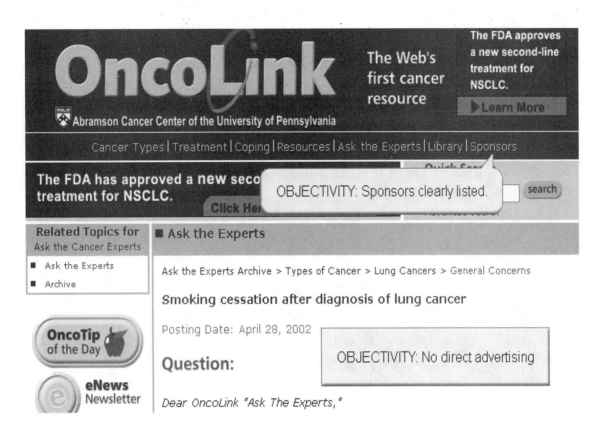

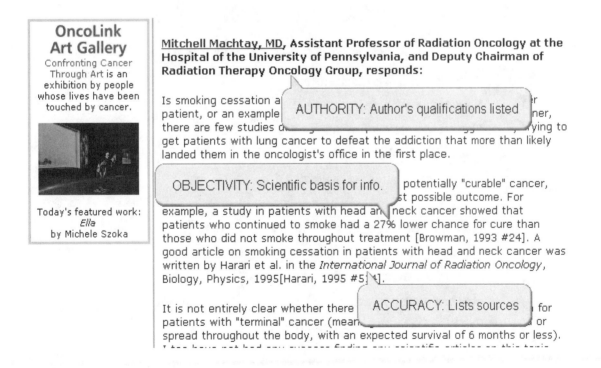

Problems with Web Page Authority & Accuracy

Potential problems with Web page authority:

- ☑ Often difficult to determine authorship of Web resources
- ☑ If author's name is listed, his/her qualifications frequently absent
- ☑ Publisher responsibility often not indicated
- ☑ Contact information often not listed

Potential problems with Web page accuracy:

- ☑ Almost anyone can publish on the Web
- ☑ Many Web resources not verified by editors or fact checkers
- ☑ Lies, inaccuracies, distortions, myths, dubious data, stereotypes
- ☑ No links to outside sources for additional information

Problems with Web Page Currency & Objectivity

Potential problems with Web page currency:

- ☑ No dates on Web pages
- ☑ May present stale information
- ☑ May be dead links
- ☑ Factual information often not dated

Potential problems with Web page objectivity:

- ☑ May advocate one point of view (bias)
- ☑ Failure to differentiate advocacy vs. fact
- ☑ May be difficult to determine goals/aims of site sponsor
- ☑ Can be means of advertising (infomercial)

Widener University, Wolfgram Memorial Library

Don't forget to DIAL

Quality Information from the Internet

Document:

Verify factual accuracy

Can it be corroborated by you or others?

Is there scholarly support for assertions?

Check the Format and Tone

Is it well-organized and easily navigated?

Is there an overt (or covert) bias, advocacy purpose or other hidden agenda?

Institution or Sponsor:

What is the reputation of the sponsor(s) or affiliated organization(s)?

Check their identity if you have a question about the site

Use **Whois** for ownership information at

http://www.networksolutions.com/whois

Author(s):

How is the author qualified to write on the subject?

Check for credentials and accessibility (e-mail or other contact information)

Linkage or Affiliations:

<u>Overt:</u> Outgoing links and/or advertisements found on the page

<u>Covert:</u> Incoming links (Use **Google or Yahoo** and simply type **link:** followed by the URL in the <u>searchbox</u>. You will be given a list of all **incoming links** and much more about the site)

What other sites exist by the same author(s) or sponsoring organization(s)?

DIAL-A-SCORE
Credibility Factors for Internet Resources

Assume that the document <u>does</u> contain the information you need; evaluate it terms of <u>quality</u>, using these criteria listed below.

NOTE: Each team may report only one score for each criteria. <u>Suggested</u> questions are *italicized*. Do not limit your scoring to these; each website is different and may require a unique approach to its evaluation.

URL:

Document:
Can the factual accuracy be corroborated by you or others? Is there scholarly or other support for assertions made? When was it written?

Confidence in Factual Accuracy

Least			**Most**	
1	2	3	4	5

### Bias or Hidden Agenda	### Site Navigation and Organization

Obvious			**Lacking**		**Difficult**			**Easy, Clear**
1	2	3	4	5	1	2	3	4	5

Institution or Sponsor:
What is the reputation of the sponsor(s) or affiliated organization(s)? What other sites do these groups sponsor?

Reputation of Sponsor

Doubtful			**Highly Respected**	
1	2	3	4	5

Author(s):
How is the author qualified to write on the subject? Check for credentials and accessibility (e-mail or other contact information). What other sites has she created?

Authority of Author(s)

Least			**Most**	
1	2	3	4	5

Linkage or Affiliations:
*Check the outgoing links and/or advertisements found on the actual page. In addition, what pages link **TO** the site? (See DIAL handout for instructions)*

Linkage Relationships/Site Affiliations

Doubtful			**Highly Respected**	
1	2	3	4	5

TOTAL _____   Michael Hunter 8/09 © 2007 Hobart and William Smith Colleges

Evaluating Internet Sites

A Guide to Avoiding the Web Sites Your Librarian Warned You About

 **Is It Real...**

Or Is It Fake?

There are two facts about the Internet you need to remember: First, not everything can be found on the Internet. Second, not everything that can be found on the Internet is accurate and true. Quality control is next to zero and deciding if a site is reliable is completely up to you. Does this mean the Internet is evil and should be avoided? Of course not! There are times when the Internet is an invaluable resource for information. The key is to only use sites you know are reliable. Remember, no one monitors the Internet for accuracy. This means that anyone can post whatever information they want -- true or untrue. So how do you decide if a site is reliable? Here are some tips:

Accuracy

Make sure the site doesn't contain grammatical, spelling, or typographical **errors**. Someone who is careless in the presentation of his site probably didn't go to much trouble to verify that the information presented is accurate.

Look to see if the author provides **sources** for the information he presents. A lack of references or citations could mean the information isn't from reliable sources.

Authority

Does the website clearly indicate who created its **content**, and does it give information on who this person or organization is? Is the creator respected in the subject area? What are his or her **credentials**? For example, I use the ESPN website to find out the latest baseball scores. It's up-to-the-minute (current), and it's affiliated with a respected company -- so I can be sure it's accurate. But would I use "Bob's Baseball Site" to look up scores? No, because Bob could update his site everyday with fake scores.

Is there **contact information** on the page for the author? The more contact information provided, the better. Look for a telephone number or physical address, not just an email address.
Also, remember that the **domain name** is not always a good indication of authority. For example just because a page is in a ".edu" domain doesn't mean it's an official college or university website. It could be a student or professor's personal page. And don't automatically trust official looking domain names. Neither the web address www.whitehouse.org or www.whitehouse.net is the official White House website.

Objectivity

Beware of **bias**! This is one of the greatest dangers in using free and non-reviewed websites for your research. Many websites are created with a specific agenda -- sometimes obvious, sometimes hidden. If I were writing a paper on gun control, would I rely exclusively on the National Rifle Association's website www.nra.org for my information? No, because information on their website would be presented with the intent on convincing me that gun control was a bad thing. The web address www.martinlutherking.org seems like it would be a good source of information on the civil rights leader. That is until you discover that the site is actually maintained by a white supremacist group.

Look for **advertising** on the page. Could the type and number of sponsors be an indication of some type of bias? The site could actually be trying to sell or promote a certain product or service.

Currency

When was the site **created**? When was its content last **updated**? Just as the copyright date in a book is important, so is the date a website was created or updated. If the site you are using doesn't have a date on it, don't use it. Likewise, if it appears it hasn't be updated in several years, be wary of using it.

Practice What You've Learned

Now look at the sites below and compare them with the tips I've just given you for deciding the reliability of a website. You'll quickly see that even though some sites seem to meet all the criteria, they're not reliable!
www.genochoice.com
Would you like to genetically design your child? You can at this website. A very realistic site -- only the topic would make you question it. If you click on "credits" you find that the creator is an artist named Virgil Wong. This site is actually a part of larger, equally well designed site, www.rythospital.com. On this site you can learn about male pregnancy and a mouse that has been implanted with human brain cells.
http://news.bbc.co.uk/2/hi/health/2284783.stm
Did you know that blondes will become extinct in about 200 years? That's according to a study done by the World Health Organization. Yes, this is a real story, on the real BBC website, and was also reported in several British papers. It was even picked up by papers in the U.S. as well as *Good Morning America*. When people began to question it, the source could not be determined. WHO stated their organization never conducted such a study. The British media claimed to have picked it up from a European news wire, but its exact source could never be traced. While the website is real, it illustrated why journals are more reliable sources than newspapers or magazines.
www.dhmo.org
Do you realize the dangers of dihydrogen monoxide? Should it be banned? This site will give

you all the details you need to make an informed decision. It contains many of the elements which make a reliable website, but it's a spoof. If you don't get the joke, don't feel bad -- it took me a while to figure it out!

So what kind of sites should you use when doing research on the web? Her are a few examples:

www.lii.org "Librarians' Internet Index " is a subject directory of internet sites. Unlike Yahoo! or Google, the sites are selected, screened, and reviewed by librarians and other subject experts.

www.census.gov The U.S. Census Bureau's website is full of statistics and demographics on the American population and economy.

www.sciway.net The South Carolina Information Highway is an excellent directory of information about South Carolina.

Some Final Points to Remember

► Most information found on the Internet can also be found in books, magazines, and journals. If you do decide to use non-reviewed Internet sites as sources for your research, you must carefully evaluate each site for reliability.

► While the Internet can be a good resource for information, it is usually not the best source. For example, if you need a research study in psychology, searching the *PsychINFO* database would be a better choice than searching the Internet. Dacus Library subscribes to almost 100 databases that provide much more scholarly information than you'll ever find by using an Internet search engine.

► If a professor tells you not to use Internet sources, that doesn't mean you can't use our databases such as *InfoTrac*. These are simply electronic versions of journal indexes that happen to be delivered to us via the Internet.

► If you're ever unsure about whether a source is reliable, call or stop by the reference desk and a librarian will be glad to help you decide.

Lynchburg College

Web Site Evaluation Score Card

Points listed in parentheses are the <u>maximum</u> to award for each characteristic.
Partial point awards are allowed: If the information listed is available, but how to get to it from the first page is not readily apparent, then assign fewer points.

Title of Web Site:

URL:

Authority

1. Individual or organization responsible for the information on the web site is clearly identified. (20 points if on first page, 20 points if on an "about us" type page, no more than 10 points if elsewhere)(Up to 20 pts)
    pts:
2. Organization, institution or individual goals clearly stated on first page or easily accessible from first page. (up to 10 pts)
    pts:
3. The author:
    a. is a faculty member at a college or university (6pts)
        pts:
    b. holds a PhD in the subject area, but is employed by a government agency or private research firm (4 pts)
        pts:
    c. presents other substantiated academic credentials (2 pts)
        pts:
    d. is an organization ***and*** there are easily indentified links to information about the staff and board of directors and their credentials (up to 6 pts)
        pts:
4. If the author is an individual, he/she has published books and or journal articles published by reputable publishers. (Search for the author in WorldCat or in an appropriate subject-specific library e-resource)(up to 4 pts)
    pts:
5. There is information to verify the legitimacy of the author or organization. A street address, phone number ***and*** e-mail address is given. (8 pts) E-mail only: (4pts)
    pts:
6. Is the copyright to the material on the page in the name of the author or organization indentified in question 1? (3 pts)
    pts:

Accuracy

7. Sources for factual information are clearly given so that they can be verified. (8 pts) If there are links to the sources, but they are not explicitly identified then give it (4pts)
    pts:

8. No obvious spelling or typographical errors. (1 pts)
    pts:

Objectivity

9. Individual or organizational bias is clearly presented. Information is not presented in a way that appeals primarily to emotions, or that purposefully attempts to mislead the reader. (10)
    pts:
10. No advertisements. (10 pts)
    pts:
11. If advertisements are present, they are clearly delineated from the information content and do not distract unduly. (up to 6 pts)
    pts:
12. Visual elements, video or graphics, enhance the information presented without resorting to emotional or psychological manipulation. (up to 5 pts)
    pts:

Currency

13. Dates are clearly given (4pts)
    pts:
14. Dates indicate that the information is kept current (3 pts)
    pts:
15. Links to outside pages are working (up to 3 pts)
    pts:

    Sub-Total for 1 – 15:

Design elements (add these points in if the total for numbers 1-15 equals at least 50.

16. Links to other pages on the site are clear and consistent. Link(s) to return to the home page are on every page and clearly identified. Navigation guides, such as breadcrumbs are used as well as site navigation guides either in tabs across the top or lists in the left column are used. (up to 8 pts)
    pts:
17. Color and texture of background and text do not detract from legibility and "white space" is used to enhance readability. (5 pts)
    pts:

Total points: 90-100+ = A, 80–89 = B, 70-79 = C, 60–69 = D, 59 or less = F

Grade:

Lynchburg College, 1501 Lakeside Drive, Lynchburg, VA

Bucknell University

Rubric for Evaluating Websites (based on form developed by T. Mills Kelly)

Your name: _____

Website url: _____

Date of your review: _____

Use the following criteria to evaluate websites:

Authority
1. Who is responsible for the contents of the page?

2. Authority rating on a scale of 1-5 (with 5 being the most authoritative)

1 2 3 4 5
3.
Are sources for factual information clearly presented so they can be verified in another source?

4. Accuracy rating on a scale of 1-5 (with 5 being the most accurate)

1 2 3 4 5
Objectivity
5. If there is advertising on the page, is it clearly differentiated from the informational content?

6. If there is a political/ideological/religious or other agenda, is it clearly stated?

7. Objectivity rating on a scale of 1-5 (with 5 being the most objective)

1 2 3 4 5
Currency
8. When was the site created, and when was it last revised?

Quality
9. Is the information free of grammatical, spelling, and typographical errors?

10. Quality rating on a scale of 1-5. (with 5 being highest quality)

1 2 3 4 5

Additional comments about this website:

BUCKNELL UNIVERSITY

701 Moore Avenue
Lewisburg, PA 17837

Online Tutorials_

SPU Library

search   EVALUATING WEBSITES – *INTRODUCTION*

How do you know if the information found on the Internet is good quality, authoritative information, or garbage? In this tutorial you will learn how to evaluate web pages for quality. It will take about 10 minutes to complete. Follow the **4 Steps** shown below.

STEP 1: THE 5 Ws
The Washington State Library recommends using **5 Ws: WHO, WHAT, WHEN, WHERE, & WHY.**

WHO is responsible for the site? Is there an author? If so, what are his/her credentials? Is the 'author' an organization or association?

WHAT type of site is it? The web site's URL address will have one of the following abbreviations to identify the type of site: .edu = educational; .org = organization; .gov = government; .com = commercial; .net = network/utilities; .mil = military

WHEN was the site created or updated? An automated date does not indicate when the information was updated.

WHERE can you find more information? Is there contact information other than an e-mail address? Is there documentation for factual statements made? Are there links to other viewpoints, if applicable?

WHY was the site created? Is the goal to sell? To persuade? To advocate an agenda? To inform? Why are advertisements (if any) there? Do they relate to the site?
Look at the two videos below to compare two different websites on the topic of AIDS according to the **5 Ws**.

STEP 2: *UNAIDS: Fast Facts* - 4:15 minutes
Click here to view presentation (video tutorial)

Here is a link to this web site, in case you want to explore it yourself.
http://www.unaids.org/en/knowledgecentre/resources/fastfacts/

STEP 3: AIDS FACTS - 2:58 minutes
Click here to view presentation (video tutorial)

Here is a link to this web site, in case you want to explore it yourself.
http://www.ithaca.edu/library/research/AIDSFACTS.htm

STEP 4: PROVIDING FEEDBACK

We would like to know what you learned from this tutorial. Please click on the link below and fill out a quick 30 second survey, to let us know if the information covered was relevant and helpful.
Evaluating Websites Feedback

Name: [   ]   **Date:** [   ]

Discerning the quality of a website can be a complicated business, but it is often worth the extra time it takes to find information that is relevant, accurate, timely, and representative of key perspectives on a given topic.

The following exercise asks you to visit, analyze, and write about two prescribed websites related to the issue of censorship. Your answers, while brief, should be as complete and thoughtful as possible. As you evaluate the sites, try to be objective before you draw your conclusions.

Type your answers into this document. When complete, print it out and hand it in to your EN 12 professor.
Important Note: Once you begin typing your answers into the exercise, you won't be able to save them. If you cannot complete the exercise within one sitting, then print out what you have and handwrite the remainder.

Website 1	**Website 2**
Am. Soc. for Defense of Tradition, Family, & Property	**Project Censored**
http://www.tfp.org/	**http://www.projectcensored.org**

1. **Who is the intended audience (e.g. women, customers, concerned citizens, etc.) and what is the nature of the site (e.g. commercial, civic, scholarly, etc.) in relation to that audience?**

Intended audience: Intended audience:

[   ]   [   ]

Nature of site in relation to audience: Nature of site in relation to audience:

[   ]   [   ]

2. **Explore the site and view a variety of entries. Is information attributed to the author(s) by name? What can you discern about the expertise or affiliation of the author(s)?**

Attribution by name (generally)? Select: Attribution by name (generally)? Select:

○ Y   or   ○ N   ○ Y   or   ○ N

What is the authors' experience/affiliation: What is the authors' experience/affiliation:

[   ]   [   ]

3. **Does the majority of information appear to be accurate? Are the arguments valid? How did you arrive at that analysis?**

Accuracy. Select your closest estimate, 1-5:   Accuracy. Select your closest estimate, 1-5:

○ ○ ○ ○ ○   ○ ○ ○ ○ ○
(Least accurate) 1 2 3 4 5 (Most accurate) (Least accurate) 1 2 3 4 5 (Most accurate)
Why?   Why?

[   ]   [   ]

Validity. Select your closest estimate, 1-5:   Validity. Select your closest estimate, 1-5:

○ ○ ○ ○ ○   ○ ○ ○ ○ ○
(Least valid) 1 2 3 4 5 (Most valid)   (Least valid) 1 2 3 4 5 (Most valid)
Why?   Why?

[   ]   [   ]

4. **Who is the publisher and what kind of entity is it (a corporation, a government agency, an advocacy group, an educational institution, an individual, etc.)? Who sponsors, or funds, publication of the site?**

Name of publisher/Kind of entity:

Name of publisher/Kind of entity:

Name of sponsor:

Name of sponsor:

How is it funded?

How is it funded?

5. **How current is the information presented? Does the site allow access to an archive of older material? What is the time span?**

Currency:

Currency:

Archive available? Select:

○ Y   or   ○ N

Archive available? Select:

○ Y   or   ○ N

Time span (4-digit year-4-digit year):

Time span (4-digit year-4-digit year):

6. **Whose point of view is presented? Can you easily identify the site's bias(es)? If so, based on what evidence?**

Whose point of view?

Whose point of view?

Bias toward:

Bias toward:

Bias against:

Bias against:

Evidence:

Evidence:

7. **Where would you look to verify, refute, or further investigate this information? Name a minimum of two different sources, and briefly explain why.**

To verify or refute:

To verify or refute:

For further investigation:

For further investigation:

8. **Briefly explain how these two websites differ from one another, yet relate to the issues of censorship and freedom of speech. Are there any notable similarities between them?**

Differences in regards to issue of censorship/freedom of speech:

Notable similarities:

Print Form

Other Web Tools

Subject Guide: Biology

| Home | Books | Databases | Journals | Class Guides | Associations | Websites |

■ My Delicious Tags

academia acting agency agriculture analysis animals anthropology art articles arts association biodiversity biology botany business chemical chemistry classification climate communication community conflict conservation countries cross_cultural dance data database demographics dialogue earth ecology education ejournal employment encyclopedia engineering english environment environmental environmental_health environmental_history environmental_issues evolution flora funds geography gis government green group health history information international journal journalism justice law literature maps mass math mathematics mediation medical medicine meteorology musicals mutual naturalhistory nature news nursing online organization physics plants playwright political politics reference research resources science search shakespeare socialwork society sociology speech statistics stocks sustainability taxonomy technical technology theatre travel world

■ I am BlackwellLibrary on Delicious

⊕ Add me to your network

Websites

Agronomy & Horticulture 100 Plant Images: Created and maintained by the Department of Agronomy and Horticulture, Brigham Young University, this site includes a JPEG gallery of approximately 150 economically important plants. Images may be used for noncommerical purposes.

AgNIC Home Page: AgNIC (Agriculture Network Information Center) is a distributed netowrk of agriculture-related information, subject area experts, and other resources. It was established by an alliance of the National ...

Salisbury
UNIVERSITY
Delicious Biology links

Bioneers | Bioneers

The Paleontology Portal: Home

Mammal Species of the World

Tree of Life Web Project

Animal Diversity Web

How to Use Google Scholar

What is Google Scholar?

Through Google Scholar, you can search for scholarly literature, including journal articles, theses, books, preprints, abstracts, conference proceedings, and technical reports.

a. Advantage

Google Scholar gets its content by crawling the web for scholarly materials (open access materials) as well as by getting information directly from publishers, including some of the resources to which the Tufts Libraries subscribe. Google Scholar, therefore, is useful for searching online journal collections such as *JSTOR, Project Muse, ScienceDirect*, and other restricted-access sources.

b. Disadvantage

Google Scholar only searches a fraction of the published scholarly literature. Compare searches in discipline standard databases *MLA, Art Abstracts, PsycINFO, MedLine, EconLit, ERIC, Engineering Villiage* and many more.

c. Caveat

For the serious researcher, Google Scholar should be used along with other key library sources.

- Databases with regular cycles of updates (It can't be determined if materials included in Google Scholar are updated from publishers on a regular, known cycle yet; some data may be out of date.)

- Databases with more specialized subject/discipline focus and powerful search capabilities.

    For example, only a database such as *Early English Books Online* will provide users with access to over 125,000 titles, comprising all known English language books from the beginning of printing to 1700

- Print indexes (to publications, for which there is no online access).

- Google Scholar does not index the library's catalog, which means that it does not provide information on every book on the library's shelves.

Get started!

General searching

- Use ~ for synonyms or related words. **~psychoanalysis** searches for *psychoanalysis, psychoanalytic,* etc.
- Use **quotation marks** " " when searching for exact phrases.

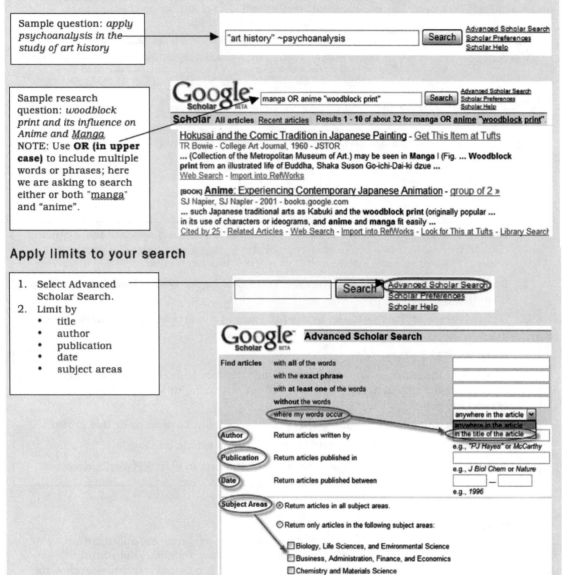

Sample question: *apply psychoanalysis in the study of art history*

Sample research question: *woodblock print and its influence on Anime and Manga.*
NOTE: Use **OR (in upper case)** to include multiple words or phrases; here we are asking to search either or both "manga" and "anime".

Apply limits to your search

1. Select Advanced Scholar Search.
2. Limit by
   - title
   - author
   - publication
   - date
   - subject areas

Search results
Ranking

Google Scholar aims to sort articles the way researchers do, weighing the full text of each article, the author, the publication in which the article appears, and how often the piece has been cited in other scholarly literature. The most relevant results will always appear on the first page.

Scholar All articles - Recent articles[1] Results **1 - 10** of about **4,890** for "**art history**" ~**psychoanalysis**. (0.09 seconds)

All Results
4.
K Salen
S Hall
S Freud
J Klein
E Zimmerman

[BOOK] Leonardo, **Psychoanalysis & Art History**: A Critical Study of Psychobiographical Approaches to
BI Collins - 1997 - Northwestern University Press
Cited by 13 - Related Articles - Web Search - Import into RefWorks - Look for This at Tufts[2] - Library Search

The State of Psychoanalytic Research in **Art History** - Get This Item at Tufts[3]
J Spector - The Art Bulletin, 1988 - JSTOR
... very few psychologists are interested in this field."6 A more explicit rejection
of the cooperation between art history and psychoanalysis was formulated by ...
5 Cited by 13 6 Related Articles 7 Web Search Import into RefWorks 8.

---

1. **Recent Articles** – Sorts your results so that newer research appears more quickly, considering factors like the prominence of the author's and journal's previous papers, full text of each article and how often it has been cited.

2. **Look for this at Tufts** – Searches the Tufts Catalog for books; link to Interlibrary Loan (ILLiad)

3. **Get this item at Tufts** – Links to the full texts of the article, search for print copy in your library, and link to Interlibrary Loan (ILLiad).

4. **More works** by the authors

5. **Cited By** – Identifies other works (only those that are indexed in Google Scholar) that have cited this article. (Compare citation searching in *Web of Science* and *Scopus*.)

6. **Related Articles** – Finds other papers that are similar to articles in this group.

7. **Web Search** – Searches for information about this article on Google.

8. **Import into RefWorks** – Allows you to save citations to your RefWorks account.

More Help

About Google Scholar	http://scholar.google.com/intl/en/scholar/about.html
General Help	http://scholar.google.com/intl/en/scholar/help.html
Advanced Search Tips	http://scholar.google.com/intl/en/scholar/refinesearch.html

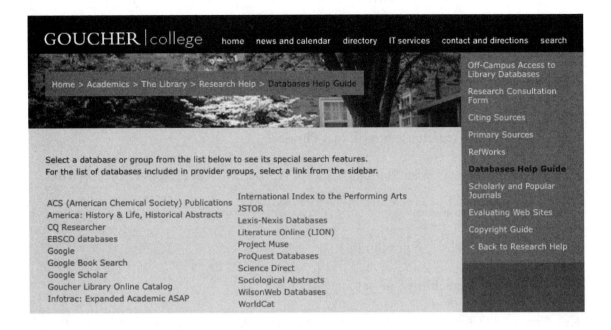

Google

Optimal Search Template: Advanced (to right of simple box)

Default Connector: AND and OR when using simple box (ANDed sites ranked higher.) To phrase-search use box "Exact Phrase."

Possible Connectors: Use "with all" box for **AND**s. Use "at least one" box for **OR**s.

strong>Truncation: no truncation

Proximity Searching: no proximity except phrase

Formal Subject Searching: no subject searching

Key Features:

- Occurrences drop-down menu: Select "in title of page."
- Domain: Can fill in ".edu" etc.

Google Book Search

Optimal Search Template: Advanced (to right of simple box)

Default Connector: AND and OR when using simple box (ANDed sites ranked higher.) To phrase-search use box "Exact Phrase."

Possible Connectors: Use "with all" box for **AND**s. Use "at least one" box for **OR**s.

Truncation: no truncation

Proximity Searching: no proximity

Formal Subject Searching: no subject searching

Key Feature: "Search in this book" input box (to right of page images).

Google Scholar

Optimal Search Template: Advanced (to right of simple box)

Default Connector: AND and OR when using simple box (ANDed sites ranked higher.) To phrase-search use box "Exact Phrase."

Possible Connectors: Use "with all" box for **AND**s. Use "at least one" box for **OR**s

Truncation: no truncation

Proximity Searching: no proximity

Formal Subject Searching: no subject searching

Key Feature:"@ my library" links provide quick full text or other paths to obtaining item.

GOOGLE TRIVIA: Founded by two Stanford grad students, incorporated in Sept. 1998 – housed in a friend's garage. (WWW was only released in 1992.) The web is now searched worldwide at a rate of over a million searches per minute; 60% of searches via Google.

GENERAL GOOGLE SEARCH TIPS

- **Exact phrase**: use quotation marks, E.g., "Messiah College students"
- **PowerPoint slides**: add ppt to search, E.g., plagiarism ppt
- **Images only**: click on "Images" above the Google search box and search
- **Definitions**: type "define:" prior to word or phrase. E.g., define: apotheosis [include the colon after "define"]
- **Synonyms**: Put tilde sign (~) directly in front of word. E.g., ~simple

ADVANCED GOOGLE SEARCHING

- **Limit by language**
- **Eliminate words** (best tip!)
- **Domain** (E.g., .edu)
- **Date range, country, etc**. [click on "+" link at bottom of Advanced screen]

SOME OTHER GOOGLE FEATURES

- **Weather**: weather 17027
- **Time**: time Baghdad (use city, town, or small country)
- **Local searches (city/town):** E.g., pizza Grantham, PA; furniture Mechanicsburg, PA
- **Stocks**: Key in stock symbol. E.g., hsy (for Hershey)
- **Movies:** Key in: movies. In first result, click on "change location" and key in your zip code.
- **Package/vehicle/flight tracking, etc.:** Just key in a UPS or FedEx tracking number, a Vehicle ID number (VIN), UPC code, airline with flight number, etc.
- **Phone number with map:** Key in phone number (with the area code). Click on link & you will able to get a map OR delete access to your information.
- **Street view maps:** Key in street address city and state. Click on the orange ball & explore!
- **Google calendar:** View your own & your family members' schedules (under More/Even more)

NEWS

- Click on **News** link at top of Google screen for current news.
- Key in terms, E.g, Barack Obama or Messiah College
- Create **News Alert** (see bottom left column) for new you wish to track
- **Advanced News Search**: Specify news source, E.g., CNN, New York Times
SEE: http://www.google.com/intl/en/help/features.html for listing & help additional types of searches

HEALTH CONCERNS

Try Microsoft's new search engine: **Bing.com** which breaks down info. by symptoms, diagnosis, prognosis, etc.

Go to http://google.com and click on the "more" link above Google search box; select "Scholar" OR from the Messiah Library homepage, select Articles/Databases, then Google Books in the General column.

What can I search in Google Scholar?
Google Scholar searches academic publishers, professional societies, preprint repositories and universities, and journal publishers available across the web for scholarly materials such as:
• **peer-reviewed** papers and journal articles
• theses
• books
• technical reports

Will I be able to read the full text of what I find?
Some of the content is available in full text, while in some instances abstracts with links to pay-for document delivery services are displayed.
NOTE: If articles from Messiah College databases are listed, Google will direct users (on-campus) to the article. See Google Books below for directions on locating books.

HOW TO: Link to Messiah College Library Resources from Google Scholar

1. Search for topic
2. Look for **"Full Text @ Library"**, or **"Library Search"** links
3. Click on the links, and they will take you to the full text of journal articles, or the catalog record of books that are in the library

Examples:
The West: Unique, Not Universal - Full-Text @ My Library - all 5 versions »
SP Huntington - Foreign Affairs, 1996 - foreignaffairs.org
... a **culture**, however, involves language, **religion**, values, traditions ... significantly altering the basic **culture** of the ... that the spread of pop **culture** and consumer ...
Cited by 70 - Related Articles - Web Search - BL Direct

[BOOK] Why **God** Won't Go Away: Brain **Science** and the Biology of Belief
AB Newberg, GDA Eugene, V Rause - 2001 - secweb.org
... observations to support a theory shared by Matthew Alper in "The **God** Part of ... so much direct study into the brain and the process of **religion** in the ... Bad **Science** ...
Cited by 88 - Related Articles - Cached - Web Search - Library Search

Go to http://google.com and click on the "more" link above Google search box; select "Books."
OR from the Messiah Library homepage, select Articles/Databases, then Google Books in the
General column.

What can I search in Google Books?
Search the bibliographic record, table of contents and often the full text of books that have been
entered by libraries and publishers into Google Books.

What will I see when I 'open' a book?
Depending on copyright or publisher permissions, you may be able to preview pages, or read the
entire book. In other cases, you will only get bibliographic information with links to purchase or
borrow the book.

How can I locate or borrow a book I find in Google Books?
After going to the book view, click on the "Find this Book in a Library" or "Find Libraries" link.
The menu in the right margin may look something like this:

Buy This Book
Yale University Press - Publisher
Amazon.com
Barnes&Noble.com - $27.00

Find this book in a library:
Scroll down to the Libraries tab to see a list of libraries that own this book.

*If you are searching from or are close to Messiah campus, and Messiah owns the book,
Messiah will be listed first. Google knows where you are (!) and will list the libraries in
geographical proximity order. If you are not geographically close to Messiah during
your search, simply type 17027 in the location information box to make Messiah the first
library listed.*

If Messiah is listed (i.e., Messiah has the book in our library collection), click on the "Messiah
College, Murray Library" link to go to our catalog. In the catalog record, you will find the call
number. Come into the library and check it out.

If Messiah is not listed, we do not have the book in our library collection. Simply select the link
in the Services line. Login to your ILLiad account using your network ID and password. Submit
the request and we will get the book for you through Interlibrary Loan.

© 2008 Messiah College

Assessment

COMPETENCY	Beginner	Novice	Proficient	Mastery
Identifies and accesses appropriate information sources to satisfy a defined need	☐ **Accesses and utilizes only open source information from search engines such as Google**	☐ **Uses academic, professional and open source information sources as selected and/or directed by faculty or librarians to meet a defined need.**	☐ **In consultation with faculty and/or librarians, utilizes a variety of discipline specific academic, professional and popular research tools and resources as well as open source search engines.**	☐ **Independently utilizes a variety of discipline specific academic, professional and popular research tools and resources as well as open source search engines.**
	☐ Search strategy is unstructured and ineffective.	☐ Demonstrates limited knowledge of Boolean, phrase and keyword search strategies	☐ Applies knowledge of Boolean, truncation, phrase, and keyword search strategies to focus the query with some consistency.	☐ Utilizes effective Boolean, truncation, phrase, keyword search, and controlled subject heading search strategies to focus the query.
	☐ Discipline specific vocabulary, concepts and structures are missing.	☐ Demonstrates limited knowledge of discipline specific vocabulary, concepts and structures	☐ Applies knowledge of discipline specific vocabulary, concepts and structures with some consistency.	☐ Consistently uses discipline specific vocabulary, concepts and structures.
	☐ Is unaware of distinctions between primary and secondary sources.	☐ Distinguishes between primary sources and secondary sources as directed.	☐ In consultation with faculty utilizes primary sources and raw data as required.	☐ Independently consults and/or creates primary sources and raw data as needed.

COMPETENCY	Beginner	Novice	Proficient	Mastery
Identifies and accesses appropriate information sources to satisfy a defined need	☐ **Limits research to one media type.**	☐ **Utilizes print, digital and other types of media sources as assigned or selected by faculty or librarians.**	☐ **Utilizes print, digital and other types of media with the limited assistance of faculty and/or librarians.**	☐ **Utilizes print, digital and other types of media in the creation of new knowledge.**
	☐ Is unaware of opportunities to obtain help from information and technology professionals when needed.	☐ Demonstrates knowledge of ways to obtain help from information and technology professionals when needed.	☐ Utilizes information and technology professionals to increase research effectiveness when needed.	☐ Actively seeks and collaborates with colleagues, information and technology professionals to increase research effectiveness and create new knowledge.
	☐ Demonstrates limited knowledge of bibliography and footnotes.	☐ Demonstrates knowledge of bibliography and footnote use to identify further information sources.	☐ Consults bibliographies and footnotes to identify further information sources with some consistency.	☐ Consistently consults bibliographies and footnotes to identify further information sources.
	☐ **Unaware of opportunities to utilize information resources outside of the home institution.**	☐ **Knowledge of access methods for information resources that exist outside of the home institution.**	☐ **With guidance from librarians and/or faculty accesses information outside of the home institution.**	☐ **Actively seeks relevant information outside of the home institution.**

Information Literacy - (Evidence from LA 100, BUS 101, ENGR 102-03)

Evidence demonstrates ability to identify and access relevant information resources in order to satisfy a specific need.

Competency	4 Thorough	3 Adequate	2 Limited	1 Weak	0 Unscored
Evidence demonstrates ability to identify and access relevant information resources in order to satisfy a specific need	Uses discipline specific academic, professional and/or open source search engines Uses effective Boolean, truncation, phrase, keyword search, and/or controlled subject heading search strategies	Uses academic, professional and/or open source search engines Applies knowledge of Boolean, truncation, phrase and/or keyword search strategies	Uses open source information and popular articles only Demonstrates limited knowledge of keyword search strategies	Uses only open source information from search engines such as Google Search strategy is unstructured and ineffective	Evidence doesn't indicate what the search strategy is

©Western New England College

Springfield College / Dakota State University

Springfield College Information Literacy across the Curriculum:
Matrix of objectives by General Education and Disciplines based on ACRL Standards

(Approved by the SC Faculty Curriculum Committee February 9, 2006)

Standard	Objective	General Education	Discipline-specific
Standard 2 The information literate student accesses needed information effectively and efficiently.	**2.1** Students will be able to distinguish between online catalogs, databases, gateways to online databases, and internet only search tools.	Students will be able to demonstrate the ability to distinguish between online catalogs, library databases, and public internet search tools. Students will have a familiarity with the library homepage and how to locate various services and information resources from it. Students will be able to understand the differences between various databases and begin to understand how to select appropriate databases for specific information needs.	Students will be able to demonstrate the ability to identify key resources and databases for a specific subject area. Students will be able to demonstrate an ability to select appropriate databases and research tools to support discipline and professional research. Students will be able to identify and use databases that will provide information about specific types of research sources such as testing instruments, dissertations, conference papers, etc.

Karl E. Mundt Library & Learning Commons
Dakota State University
820 N. Washington Avenue
Madison, SD 57042-1799

IL objectives: Bucknell University

Evaluating resources--sample outcomes

•Identify criteria for evaluating information sources in order to select resources appropriate for academic research.

•Compare and analyze website(s) based on authority, accuracy, purpose, scope, and currency in order to select resources appropriate to college-level work.

BUCKNELL UNIVERSITY
701 Moore Avenue
Lewisburg, PA

Bowdoin College
Question on Pre-test of Information Literacy:

14. If you are writing a paper on animal rights, and you use information from a web site produced by the People for the Ethical Treatment of Animals (PETA), which web site evaluation criterion/criteria should you consider?

A. Are the sources of factual information easy to verify?

B. Is there bias?

C. How current is the information?

D. What related links are provided?

E. All of the above.

Bowdoin College · Brunswick, Maine

Each search engine searches its own index of the web, so that you will get different results depending on which search engine you use.

- ○ A) True

- ○ B) False

Submit

Clear   Next

Typing *domestic violence* into Google's basic search box will display:

- ○ A) Web pages with either keyword

- ○ B) Web pages that contain both words in any order

- ○ C) Web pages that contain the phrase in the order listed

- ○ D) Web pages with either keyword, but not both

Submit   Clear

Next

If the website URL is www.irs.gov/pub/irs-pdf/fw4.pdf, you can expect you are seeing:

- ○ A) a web page from the government

- ○ B) a photograph from a college

- ○ C) a governmental printable document

- ○ D) an organization's printable form

Submit   Next

Clear

Clicking on a "sponsored link" will take you to an advertiser's website.

- ○ A) True

- ○ B) False

Submit

Clear   Next

Effective Web Searching—Quiz 1

1. Find out where Ernest Hemingway, the writer, was born. Where will you look for this answer?

2. Find out the meaning of *etymology.* Where will you look for this answer?

3. Would you find the answer to either of the above questions using the Find command or **Find** button on the browser toolbar?

4. What's an Internet domain?

5. In which domains are you likely to find the following sites?

Internal Revenue Service	.
The U.S. Navy	.
Pepsi	.
Harvard University	.
CNN	.
NPR or PBS	.
MLA	.
Primus Internet Service Provider	.

6. What is a "search string" and is this an example (below)?

museum paris impressionist

7. If you're currently using the Google search engine, how would you switch to Yahoo?

8. If you want to return to a site you visited 30 minutes ago, what is the best way to get back there?

9. What are the problems (3) with typing the following URL (on left) in the Location field (on right)?
http;//www.itn

http://www.bu.edu/celop/mll/index.html

10. *Without* actually following the link, what do you think the following URL is for?

www.royal.gov.uk

11. What happens if you have visited 5 sites in a linear fashion then click the Forward button?

12. What's the easiest way to get to the main B.U. page if you are at the following page?

http://www.bu.edu/celop/mll/students/index.shtml

13. What would be the most efficient way to find images of a raccoon?

14. How do you save a copy of an image you like from a Web page?

Answers to Effective Web Searching—Quiz 1

EFFECTIVE Web searches require conscious decisions made *before* the search. Think about *where* to look for information, where it *should* be found. Using a search engine, such as Google or Yahoo, is only one of the options—and not always the best one. Approach the search for information on the Web as you would approach this search in the world outside the Web. If you want to know the current price of gold, go to the business section of a newspaper. Using the Web, go to the online version. If you want to know where Pablo Picasso was born, go to an encyclopedia because this is a static fact. Using the Web, go to the Encyclopedia Britannica available from the B.U. Web site. Don't look for this kind of information using a search engine. Also, know your **sources**. Just because you found information on the Web, doesn't mean it's accurate. Anyone can put anything on a Web page.

1. Find out where Ernest Hemingway, the writer, was born. Where will you look for this answer?
(Almost all students give "1899" as the answer. But the question is **where**, not **when**.) He was born in Oak Park, Illinois. Use Encyclopedia Britannica from the B.U. Web site (Tools and Resources) for this kind of static fact. There are other, free encyclopedias also, such as Columbia. Type his name into the search field and you will find a short biography. Other sites, such as A&E's Biography.com also offer short biographical information. Do not trust the information found on "fan" pages. Find a reputable, known source.

2. Find the meaning of *etymology*. Where will you look for this answer?

You're looking for the definition of a word. Use a dictionary. Several free online dictionaries are listed on the **Dictionaries** pop-up menu on the MLL Students' page. *Etymology* is the study of word origins. The best source for word origins is the Oxford English Dictionary (OED) from the B.U. Web site. Many other online dictionaries, such as Merriam-Webster, offer a short note, usually sufficient, on the origin as well. They also offer an audible option where you can hear the word pronounced. Click on the speaker icon ◀️)).

3. Would you find the answer to either of the above questions using the Find on Page command or Find button?

No. The Find feature (at right) in Navigator and Explorer (**Edit** > **Find**) only searches the current page for the occurrence of the specified word, much as it would in a word processor. Using the Find command on this page would simply bring you to either of the above questions, where those words appear. This command does not perform an Internet search as a search engine does, but it's useful for finding a particular reference in text in a vary long text Web page, such as a paper.

4. What's an Internet domain?

The main (or "top level") categories of the World Wide Web. For example, .com is the commercial domain, .edu is the educational domain. *.info, .name, and .biz were added in the domain expansion to provide more addresses.

5. In which domains are you likely to find the following sites?

Internal Revenue Service	.gov
The U.S. Navy	.mil
Pepsi	.com
Harvard University	.edu
CNN	.com
NPR or PBS	.org
MLA	.org
Primus Internet service provider	.net

You might find the same domain name registered in more than one domain category. For example, there is www.navy.mil for the official U.S. Navy site, but www.navy.org is a commercial E-mail provider for Navy personnel. Often, an organization will also register the same domain name in several different domain categories simply to stake a larger claim.

6. What is a "search string" and is this an example (below)?

museum paris impressionist

Search strings are key words that define your search. You type them into a search field (below) on search engines (such as Google, Yahoo, etc.). Yes, above is an example of a search string. Generally, the above string would look for the occurrence of ANY of the words in Web pages, not all. To limit your results to pages that contain all of the words, type
museum AND paris AND impressionist
You can also put quotes around the string, which might be more effective for a search for pages having to do with "english as a second language" for example.

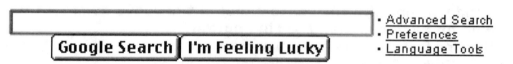

"Google Search," above, will give you results for your search. "I'm Feeling Lucky," will bring you directly to the page for the first listing in the results. The "Advanced Search" link to the right will help you narrow down your search results without getting into the use of boolean operators.

7. If you're currently using the Google search engine, how would you switch to Yahoo?

If you know the address (the URL) type it directly into the Location or

Address field. Don't type it into a search field. As an analogy, if you know your friend's phone number, do you still call 411? No, you dial his number directly. Likewise with the Web. Simply type "yahoo" in the location field and the browser will autocomplete the syntax and assume that it is in the .com domain, since the vast majority of all pages on the Web are in that domain.

8. If you want to return to a site you visited 30 minutes ago, what is the best way to get back there?

Pull down the **Go** menu (in IE) or click and hold on the **Back** button (Nav) and find the site down the list, which is in reverse chronological order (most recent on top). Note that if you're using Netscape Navigator and a link opened in a new browser window (known as "spawning" a new window), then the new window may not have the page visit history of the referring page.

9. What are the problems (3) with typing the following URL in the Location field?

http;//www.itn

1. **;** should be **:** 2. **.com** is missing. 3. **http://** is not necessary. (In fact, nothing but the domain name, itn, is necessary since this is a .com site.) **www.itn.com** is correct (simply **itn** will work in IE).

10. *Without* actually following the link, what do you think the following URL is for?

www.royal.gov.uk

uk is the country code for the United Kingdom (Great Britain); **gov** indicates a government site; **royal** suggest the monarchy. It's the British Monarchy's Web site. This question gets at the breakdown of a URL. Look at the 6 parts of a URL (uniform resource locator, or simply location) below.

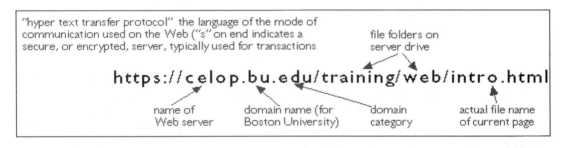

11. What happens if you have visited 5 sites in a linear fashion then click the Forward button?

Nothing. The Forward button (at right, dimmed and unavailable) only moves forward to a visited site if you have moved backwards.

12. What's the easiest way to get to the main BU page if you are at the following page?

http://www.bu.edu/celop/mll/startup/index.html

Select and delete everything after the domain category (.edu) in the URL in the Location window. Press the Return key, which should bring you to http://www.bu.edu/

13. What would be the most efficient way to find images of a raccoon?

Search engines, such as Google, have dedicated image searches where all of your results are thumbnail pictures. In Google, click on the **Images** tab to begin an image search and type in the keyword(s). Click on one to go to the source page. A dedicated image search gives only images as results, unlike a normal search, which produces text descriptions and links of HTML pages. Google probably looks at the alternative text tag information for images to match the names (pictures on Web pages can have a text description entered in the HTML code that will display only if the image does not, or while a slow-loading image downloads).

Google™
Image Search

| Web | **Images** | Groups | Directory | News-New! |

[_____] [Google Search] · Advanced Image Search
· Preferences
· Image Search Help

The most comprehensive image search on the web.

14. How do you save a copy of an image you like from a Web page?

On a Mac, place the pointer over the image and click and hold the mouse button. An options list will pop up (below). Choose, "Download Image to Disk" or "Save this image as..." or the like. Browse to the appropriate saving location on your computer. You can also choose "Copy image" and it will be copied to the clipboard so that you can paste it somewhere else, such as in a word processing document. On a PC, click the right mouse button on an image and save as above. Images that you can save or copy include .gif, .jpg, or .png formats. Some images are displayed using other technologies, such as Flash movies or Java applets. You can only capture these images through the use of a screen capture utility for your computer, which essentially allows you to draw a marquee box around any part of your screen and copy it to the clipboard or save it.

| **Back** |
| **Forward** |
| **Reload** |
| **Open this Page in Composer** |
| **Send Page...** |
| **Page Source** |
| **Page Info** |

| **Internet Explorer Help...** |
| **Open Image in New Window** |
| **Download Image to Disk** |
| **Copy Image** |
| **Reload Image** |

| **Open this Image** |
| **Copy this Image Location** |
| **Save this Image as...** |
| **Copy this Image** |
| **Load this Image** |

Pop-up menu in Internet Explorer

Pop-up menu in Netscape Navigator